W9-BGF-819

AP WORLD HISTORY FLASHCARDS

Premium Edition with CD-ROM

Test-Readiness Quizzes
with Instant Scoring

PLUS World History Timelines
for Windows®

Mark Bach
AP World History Teacher
Apex Learning
Seattle, Washington

Research & Education Association
Visit our website at: www.rea.com

Research & Education Association
61 Ethel Road West
Piscataway, New Jersey 08854
E-mail: info@rea.com

REA's Flashcard Book
for the AP World History Exam
Premium Edition with CD-ROM

Published 2012

Copyright © 2009 by Research & Education
Association, Inc. All rights reserved. No part
of this book may be reproduced in any form
without permission of the publisher.

Printed in the United States of America

Library of Congress Control Number 2008941960

ISBN 13: 978-0-7386-0504-3
ISBN 10: 0-7386-0504-2

F11-0101

About This Premium Edition with CD-ROM

REA's unique Premium Edition Flashcard Book features questions and answers to help you study for the Advanced Placement World History Exam. This book, enhanced with an interactive CD-ROM, is designed to fit conveniently into your study schedule for AP World History. You'll find it's an especially effective study tool when paired with REA's *AP World History,* our celebrated comprehensive review and practice-exam book.

This handy volume is filled with 400 must-study AP World History questions and detailed answers. Our multiple-choice questions mirror the actual AP exam format and are chronologically ordered to cover all topics found on the AP World History exam from 8000 B.C.E. to the present. The full index makes it easy to look up a particular subject and review a specific historical time period.

Unlike most flashcards that come loose in a box, these flashcards are bound in an easy-to-use, organized book. This innovative Flashcard Book lets you write your answer to a question on the front of the card, and then compare it to the answer on the back of the card. REA's flashcards are a great way to boost your test-readiness and are perfect for studying on the go.

The CD-ROM includes four test-readiness quizzes and a world history timeline the summarizes major events.

This Premium Edition Flashcard Book has been carefully developed with REA's customary concern for excellence. We believe you will find it an outstanding addition to your AP World History prep.

Larry B. Kling
Chief Editor

About the Author

Mark Bach has taught World History since 1983 and is currently an online instructor of Advanced Placement United States History with Seattle-based Apex Learning. He is a faculty consultant for the College Board and has served as an AP reader for both the U.S. History and World History exams.

Mr. Bach received his B.A. in History and German from St. Olaf College in Minnesota and his M.A. from Michigan State University. He is also on the history faculty at the International Community School in Kirkland, Washington.

About Research & Education Association

Founded in 1959, Research & Education Association (REA) is dedicated to publishing the finest and most effective educational materials—including software, study guides, and test preps—for students in middle school, high school, college, graduate school, and beyond.

We invite you to visit us at *www.rea.com* to find out how "REA is making the world smarter."

Acknowledgments

In addition to our author, we would like to thank Larry B. Kling, Vice President, Editorial, for his overall guidance, which brought this publication to completion; Pam Weston, Vice President, Publishing, for setting the quality standards for production integrity and managing the publication to completion; John Cording, Vice President, Technology, for coordinating the design and development of REA's CD software; Diane Goldschmidt, Senior Editor, for editorial project management; Alice Leonard, Senior Editor, for preflight editorial review; Heena Patel and Amy Jamison, Technology Project Managers, for their design contributions and software testing efforts; Jeff LoBalbo, Senior Graphic Designer, for coordinating pre-press electronic file mapping; and Christine Saul, Senior Graphic Designer, for designing our cover.

We also extend special thanks to Marianne L'Abbate for copyediting, Ellen Gong for proofreading, and Kathy Caratozzolo of Caragraphics for typesetting this edition.

Table of Contents

Test-Readiness Quizzes on CD

After studying questions 1 through 99, take Quiz 1.
Take Quiz 2 after studying questions 100 through 198.
After studying questions 199 through 298, take Quiz 3.
Quiz 4 starts after question 400.

Questions

Q–1

One commonality of both the Roman and Hellenistic empires was their tactics of

(A) democratic decision making
(B) military conquest and pacification
(C) transoceanic exploration
(D) missionary outreach
(E) amphibious warfare

Your Answer _____

_____

Q–2

One of the main outcomes of the Neolithic Revolution was

(A) a new vulnerability to disease
(B) a rise in local population rates
(C) new monarchies being formed
(D) a greater ability to hunt game
(E) the invention of the chariot

Your Answer _____

_____

Correct Answers

A-1

(B) Both the Macedonians and the Romans built powerful armies that facilitated the expansion of the two empires in the ancient era. Their militaries would generally engage an enemy and after defeating them, pacify the population and absorb the territory into their empire. Soldiers could often stay and colonize the new addition to the empire and participate in its rule.

A-2

(B) Sedentary agriculture gave rise to permanent communities that could stay in one place and produce food. When surpluses resulted, they made higher birthrates possible. The community could feed more people, and populations could then increase over time.

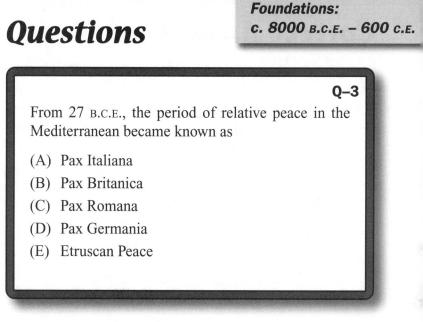

Q–3

From 27 B.C.E., the period of relative peace in the Mediterranean became known as

(A) Pax Italiana

(B) Pax Britanica

(C) Pax Romana

(D) Pax Germania

(E) Etruscan Peace

Your Answer _____

_____

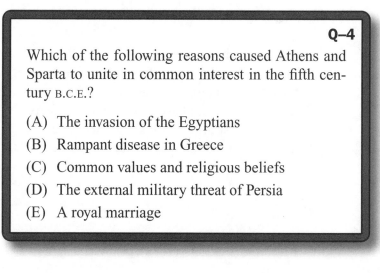

Q–4

Which of the following reasons caused Athens and Sparta to unite in common interest in the fifth century B.C.E.?

(A) The invasion of the Egyptians

(B) Rampant disease in Greece

(C) Common values and religious beliefs

(D) The external military threat of Persia

(E) A royal marriage

Your Answer _____

_____

Correct Answers

A–3

(C) The consolidation of the Roman empire under Octavian produced a period of over two centuries of stability that became known as Pax Romana, or Roman Peace. Roman law, commerce, and culture spread to northern Europe and into North Africa. Roman Caesars ruled over a vast territory that was pacified by their military and run by their civil administrators.

A–4

(D) In 479 B.C.E. the encroachment of the Persians into the Aegean helped unify some of the Greek city-states in common defense. Thirty-one Greek city-states, including Sparta and Athens, decided to resist the rule of Xerxes and defeated the Persians to maintain their independence.

Q–5

What is the correct chronology for the following eras in prehistory?

(A) Stone Age, Bronze Age, Iron Age
(B) Iron Age, Stone Age, New Stone Age
(C) Stone Age, Iron Age, Bronze Age
(D) Bronze Age, Iron Age, Stone Age
(E) Iron Age, New Stone Age, Tin Age

Your Answer _____

Q–6

Which people migrated south into ancient India and replaced the older Harappan civilization around 1500 B.C.E.?

(A) The Mughuls
(B) The Persians
(C) The Aryans
(D) The Hellenists
(E) The Mongols

Your Answer _____

Correct Answers

A–5

(A) The Paleolithic era, c. 12000 B.C.E., is the beginning of the so-called Stone Age. It was characterized by wandering clans who used stone for crude implements. With the discovery of copper and its use in combination with tin around 3500 B.C.E., more durable metal objects could be fashioned. This new alloy, bronze, could be used for both tools and weapons. Its military application and use in agriculture were significant. Around 1500 B.C.E., it is believed the Hittites discovered how to smelt iron from the raw ore found in nature. This was another advance in the fashioning of better tools and weapons in ancient times.

A–6

(C) The Aryans were originally pastoral nomads who raised cattle and domesticated horses. They came across the Hindu Kush mountains and arrived in the subcontinent of Asia, overrunning the people already living there. Recent research has reexamined the Aryan migration into South Asia, and new theories are being advanced about the origins of Vedic culture in the Indus Valley.

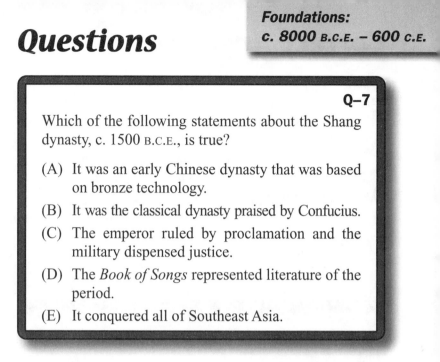

Q–7

Which of the following statements about the Shang dynasty, c. 1500 B.C.E., is true?

(A) It was an early Chinese dynasty that was based on bronze technology.

(B) It was the classical dynasty praised by Confucius.

(C) The emperor ruled by proclamation and the military dispensed justice.

(D) The *Book of Songs* represented literature of the period.

(E) It conquered all of Southeast Asia.

Your Answer _____

_____

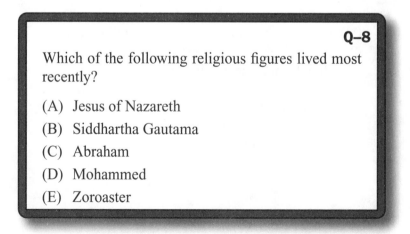

Q–8

Which of the following religious figures lived most recently?

(A) Jesus of Nazareth

(B) Siddhartha Gautama

(C) Abraham

(D) Mohammed

(E) Zoroaster

Your Answer _____

_____

Correct Answers

A–7

(A) The Shang dynasty was the earliest recorded Chinese era that rose because of its technological achievements, particularly in the area of bronze metallurgy. The agricultural dynasty grew millet and wheat, and kings managed the distribution of food to the population.

A–8

(D) Islam is the most recent world religion to be established. While Christianity, Judaism, and Buddhism came into being over 2000 years ago, Islam began around 600 C.E. on the Arabian peninsula. Mohammed was the founder of the desert religion and claimed to be the last and most important prophet.

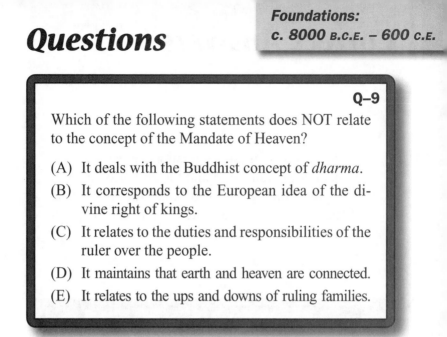

Q–9

Which of the following statements does NOT relate to the concept of the Mandate of Heaven?

(A) It deals with the Buddhist concept of *dharma*.

(B) It corresponds to the European idea of the divine right of kings.

(C) It relates to the duties and responsibilities of the ruler over the people.

(D) It maintains that earth and heaven are connected.

(E) It relates to the ups and downs of ruling families.

Your Answer _____

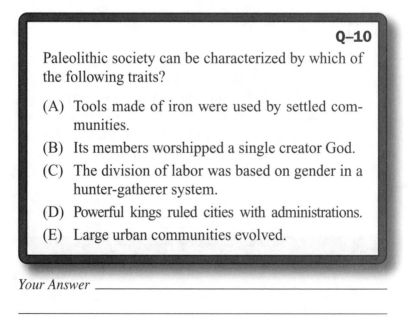

Q–10

Paleolithic society can be characterized by which of the following traits?

(A) Tools made of iron were used by settled communities.

(B) Its members worshipped a single creator God.

(C) The division of labor was based on gender in a hunter-gatherer system.

(D) Powerful kings ruled cities with administrations.

(E) Large urban communities evolved.

Your Answer _____

Correct Answers

A–9

(C) The Mandate of Heaven was first used by the Zhou dynasty to justify the takeover of the Shang dynasty. It suggested a relationship between the quality of leadership and the authority enjoyed by the ruling emperor or king. Europeans also came to believe that kings rule under the guidance of God.

A–10

(C) Social groups in the Paleolithic era grew from clans into tribes and sustained themselves through hunting and gathering food. Warfare became more organized with the use of clubs and spears. Women and men had different roles to play in finding food and preparing it.

Questions

Q–11

The earliest urban settlements are believed to have been established

(A) in North America by the Hopewell peoples

(B) by Germanic tribes in northern Europe

(C) by the Khmer clans in Southeast Asia

(D) by the Sumerians in southern Mesopotamia

(E) in the Balkans by Slavic tribes

Your Answer _____

Q–12

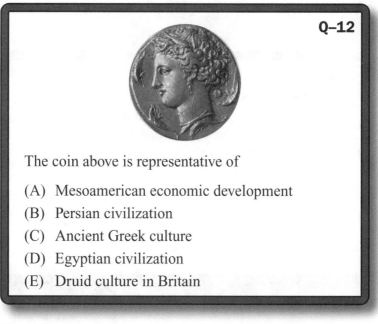

The coin above is representative of

(A) Mesoamerican economic development

(B) Persian civilization

(C) Ancient Greek culture

(D) Egyptian civilization

(E) Druid culture in Britain

Your Answer _____

Correct Answers

A–11

(D) The Sumerians established settled urban areas about 3500 B.C.E. It is theorized that they came from the Caspian Sea area. These early cities evolved into more sophisticated social orders, with government and administration.

A–12

(C) The coin shown is a *dekadrachm* coined around 400 B.C.E. in Greece. The hair and facial art are both typical of early Greek art and sculpture.

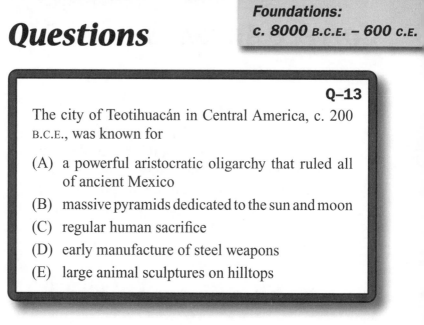

Q–13

The city of Teotihuacán in Central America, c. 200 B.C.E., was known for

(A) a powerful aristocratic oligarchy that ruled all of ancient Mexico
(B) massive pyramids dedicated to the sun and moon
(C) regular human sacrifice
(D) early manufacture of steel weapons
(E) large animal sculptures on hilltops

Your Answer _____

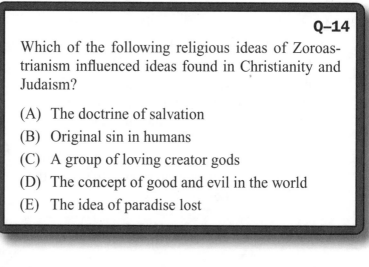

Q–14

Which of the following religious ideas of Zoroastrianism influenced ideas found in Christianity and Judaism?

(A) The doctrine of salvation
(B) Original sin in humans
(C) A group of loving creator gods
(D) The concept of good and evil in the world
(E) The idea of paradise lost

Your Answer _____

Correct Answers

A–13

(B) Teotihuacán was one of the great urban wonders of ancient America. Its pyramids were focused on worship of the heavens. It is believed to have grown to over 100,000 people by 600 C.E., and it was some 8 square miles. With no written records, all knowledge of this great city is limited to archeological excavation.

A–14

(D) Zoroaster was believed to have lived in ancient Persia c. 1200 B.C.E. He departed from the polytheistic culture of his time and proclaimed a single creator god and also evil spirits who opposed this god. He shared his teachings with his followers, and some of these ideas of one God are believed to have influenced the Hebrew monotheism that evolved around the same time period in the Levant.

Questions

Q–15

The democracy of classical Athens allowed participation only for

(A) the ruling elites
(B) free adult males
(C) male slaves and freemen
(D) the aristocracy
(E) the priestly class

Your Answer _____

_____

Q–16

What did ancient Rome and Sparta have in common?

(A) A reliance on democratic institutions
(B) Military values pervading the culture
(C) Slaves who were eventually freed by the government
(D) A single state religion
(E) Location in central Europe

Your Answer _____

_____

Correct Answers

A–15

(B) As a city-state, Athens had an early form of democracy but allowed only free males to vote in assembly. Poor farmers sometimes ended up in debt and became slaves, thus losing their political rights. This limited sharing of power by the Athenians would have some impact on Roman republican systems and a great impact on later governments in the modern era.

A–16

(B) Both Rome and Sparta had strong militaristic traditions. Young men were raised to serve as soldiers, and mothers prized the ability to bear sons. Soldiering was a prestigious profession, and one could rise in social rank based on one's service to the state.

Q–17

The Olmec, c. 1400 B.C.E., were known as

(A) a trading people who ranged across North America
(B) militarily aggressive and brutal
(C) a society without religious beliefs or rituals
(D) an early Mesoamerican society with a central authority
(E) successors to the Aztecs

Your Answer _____

Q–18

The world's first empire was created by the

(A) Akkadians, who ruled the Fertile Crescent c. 2300 B.C.E.
(B) Babylonians, who dominated what is present-day Iraq
(C) Egyptians in the Nile region in the second millennium B.C.E.
(D) Syrian peoples north of the Levant
(E) Aryans, who dominated the Hindu Kush

Your Answer _____

Correct Answers

A–17

(D) The Olmec created the first organized civilization along the Gulf Coast of America. These people formed small urban communities that shared religious practices. Giant basalt sculptures were carved with hand tools and probably represented powerful rulers.

A–18

(A) The Akkadians conquered the Sumerians and established rule beyond the Tigris and Euphrates area, from the Mediterranean to the Persian Gulf.

Questions

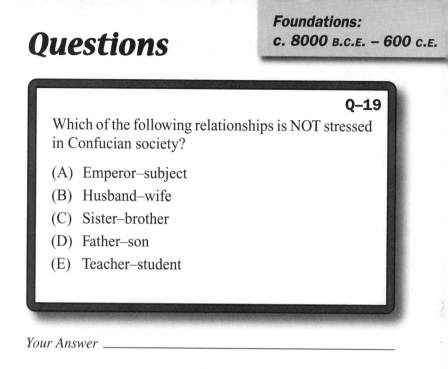

Q–19

Which of the following relationships is NOT stressed in Confucian society?

(A) Emperor–subject
(B) Husband–wife
(C) Sister–brother
(D) Father–son
(E) Teacher–student

Your Answer _____

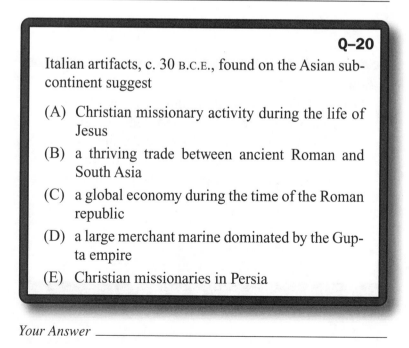

Q–20

Italian artifacts, c. 30 B.C.E., found on the Asian sub-continent suggest

(A) Christian missionary activity during the life of Jesus
(B) a thriving trade between ancient Roman and South Asia
(C) a global economy during the time of the Roman republic
(D) a large merchant marine dominated by the Gupta empire
(E) Christian missionaries in Persia

Your Answer _____

Correct Answers

A–19

(C) Confucius laid the framework for a harmonious society by suggesting that certain hierarchical relationships could stabilize the nation. These relationships suggested superior and inferior hierarchies within families and the nation as a whole. Sibling relationships involving sisters were not underscored.

A–20

(B) Ceramics and small buildings linked to ancient Rome have been excavated near present-day Madras in India. Dated around the time of Augustus, this evidence suggests that trading took place in the earliest years of the Roman empire between Rome and ancient India.

Q–21

The image above relates to

(A) Carthaginian leaders

(B) Phoenician navigation

(C) Sumerian artwork

(D) the Roman Pantheon

(E) Greek art

Your Answer _____

Correct Answers

A–21

(D) The image is that of Mercury, the Roman messenger god. He was one of several major deities worshipped in the Roman era. Gods tended to be associated with the heavens or nature. They often had personalities and were ruled by Jupiter, the lord of the gods.

Q–22

Semen est sanguis Christianorum.
— Tertullian c. 200 C.E.

"The blood of the martyrs is the seed
[of the Church]."

The above text relates to the

(A) early persecution of the Christian church by Rome
(B) soldiers who died in battle in ancient times
(C) policies of the Senate under Constantine
(D) split in the Roman Catholic Church
(E) bishops who controlled Italy

Your Answer _____

Q–23

The Four Noble Truths of Buddhism include all of the following EXCEPT

(A) Nirvana is freedom from suffering.
(B) Desire is the cause of all suffering.
(C) Reincarnation is endless suffering.
(D) Suffering is always present in life.
(E) Detachment from desire is necessary.

Your Answer _____

Correct Answers

A-22

(A) Tertullian was one of the early Christian church fathers during the time of Roman persecution. He wrote extensively about church doctrine and how believers were to relate to the pagan world around them. His commentary on Christians killed by Rome suggests that their deaths only encouraged the growth of the religion.

A-23

(C) Buddhists believe less in reincarnation than in the need to separate oneself from desire, which causes suffering. All yearning creates pain, and the path to bliss and happiness must end in nirvana or a state of ideal detachment.

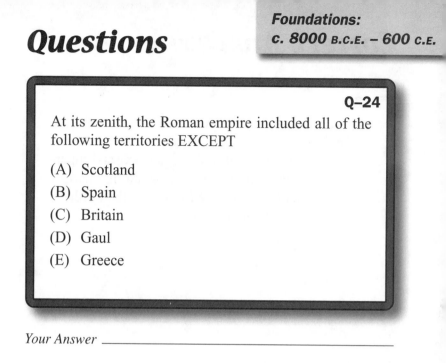

Q–24

At its zenith, the Roman empire included all of the following territories EXCEPT

(A) Scotland

(B) Spain

(C) Britain

(D) Gaul

(E) Greece

Your Answer _____

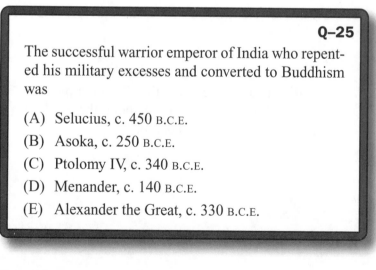

Q–25

The successful warrior emperor of India who repented his military excesses and converted to Buddhism was

(A) Selucius, c. 450 B.C.E.

(B) Asoka, c. 250 B.C.E.

(C) Ptolomy IV, c. 340 B.C.E.

(D) Menander, c. 140 B.C.E.

(E) Alexander the Great, c. 330 B.C.E.

Your Answer _____

Correct Answers

A–24

(A) The Roman empire was established in Britain but did not pacify the northern part of the island, where present-day Scotland exists. Emperor Hadrian built a wall to separate that part of Britannia controlled by Rome and the northern region held by nonpacified tribes.

A–25

(B) Asoka ruled parts of India in the third century B.C.E. and was so disheartened about one of his battles that he became a Buddhist and pacifist. He sent missionaries throughout the land to preach repentance and peace.

Q–26

The central location for Jewish worship and ritual in ancient times was the

(A) temple of Solomon in Jerusalem
(B) shrine at Masada
(C) top of Mt. Sinai
(D) banks of the river Jordan
(E) fortress of Masada

Your Answer _____

_____

Q–27

Early written evidence of China's first dynasties has been found

(A) inscribed on sandstone cliffs in Mongolia
(B) on oracle bones used for divination
(C) in buried parchments
(D) in tombs in Xian
(E) on parchments discovered in Nanjing

Your Answer _____

_____

Correct Answers

A–26

(A) The temple built by Solomon was the geographical center of Judaic worship until it was destroyed for the second time by the Romans in 70 C.E. There, the priests oversaw the national rituals of atonement and worship for the Hebrew people. The Holy of Holies housed the arc of the covenant, which dated back to the time of Moses and the Exodus. These were the most important artifacts of the early Judaic experience.

A–27

(B) The bones of birds and turtle shells were used to record religious ritual and history during the Shang dynasty. Shamans or diviners used the bones to tell the future or to determine what should be done. Questions would be posed and then hot pokers would be used to fracture the bones. The resulting cracks or breaks would then be interpreted to guide people.

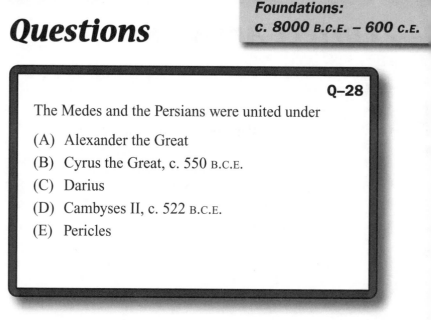

Q–28

The Medes and the Persians were united under

(A) Alexander the Great

(B) Cyrus the Great, c. 550 B.C.E.

(C) Darius

(D) Cambyses II, c. 522 B.C.E.

(E) Pericles

Your Answer _____

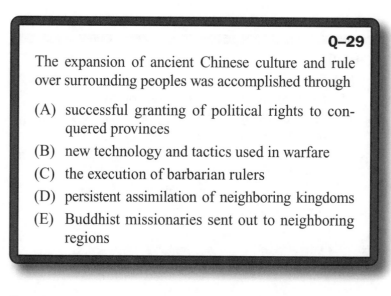

Q–29

The expansion of ancient Chinese culture and rule over surrounding peoples was accomplished through

(A) successful granting of political rights to conquered provinces

(B) new technology and tactics used in warfare

(C) the execution of barbarian rulers

(D) persistent assimilation of neighboring kingdoms

(E) Buddhist missionaries sent out to neighboring regions

Your Answer _____

Correct Answers

A-28

(B) Cyrus the Great was one of the early and successful Persian conquerors in the Middle East. Under Cyrus, the empire stretched from Persia to the Mediterranean. The nearby Medes and Lydians were incorporated into the Persian sphere and the so-called Achaemenid Empire was formed.

A-29

(D) Cultural transference often took place when Chinese dynasties conquered or were overrun themselves by neighboring peoples. Two more recent examples of the latter were the Mongols and Manchus. But even in earlier times, China would pacify and absorb so-called barbarian peoples who became culturally Chinese over time.

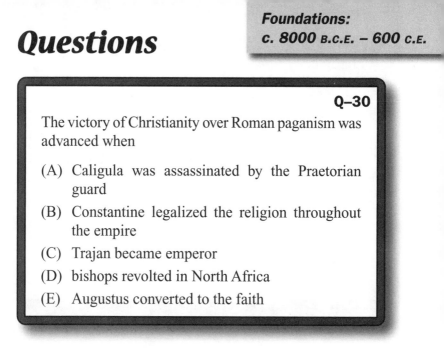

Q–30

The victory of Christianity over Roman paganism was advanced when

(A) Caligula was assassinated by the Praetorian guard

(B) Constantine legalized the religion throughout the empire

(C) Trajan became emperor

(D) bishops revolted in North Africa

(E) Augustus converted to the faith

Your Answer _____

_____

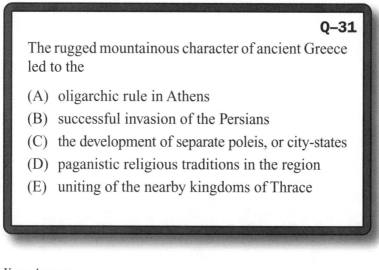

Q–31

The rugged mountainous character of ancient Greece led to the

(A) oligarchic rule in Athens

(B) successful invasion of the Persians

(C) the development of separate poleis, or city-states

(D) paganistic religious traditions in the region

(E) uniting of the nearby kingdoms of Thrace

Your Answer _____

_____

Correct Answers

A–30

(B) After having a battlefield vision of a cross in the heavens, Constantine ceased the persecution of Christians and even sponsored church councils so that early theology could be codified. A network of urban bishoprics was also established so church leadership could solidify.

A–31

(C) Greece is a peninsula covered with mountains and valleys. Communities grew up in isolation and developed their own political traditions. There were dozens of city-states, including Sparta and Athens.

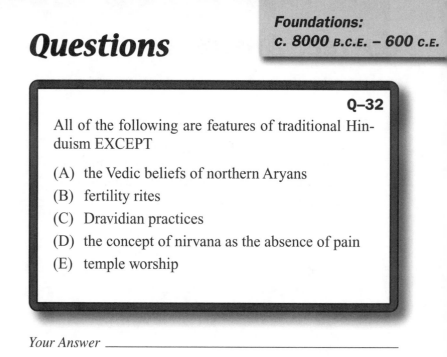

Q–32

All of the following are features of traditional Hinduism EXCEPT

(A) the Vedic beliefs of northern Aryans

(B) fertility rites

(C) Dravidian practices

(D) the concept of nirvana as the absence of pain

(E) temple worship

Your Answer _____

_____

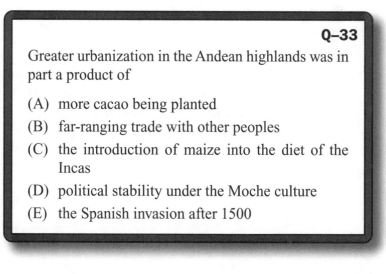

Q–33

Greater urbanization in the Andean highlands was in part a product of

(A) more cacao being planted

(B) far-ranging trade with other peoples

(C) the introduction of maize into the diet of the Incas

(D) political stability under the Moche culture

(E) the Spanish invasion after 1500

Your Answer _____

_____

Correct Answers

A–32

(D) Hinduism is a combination of religious practices that evolved over many years in South Asia. Folk religion, fertility rites, and other practices are part of the belief system. However, nirvana is a feature of Buddhist theology.

A–33

(C) Many times in world history, the introduction of a staple crop allows more people to survive into adulthood, which in turn leads to an increase of population. Maize is a hardy crop that supplies a reliable source of carbohydrates for the people.

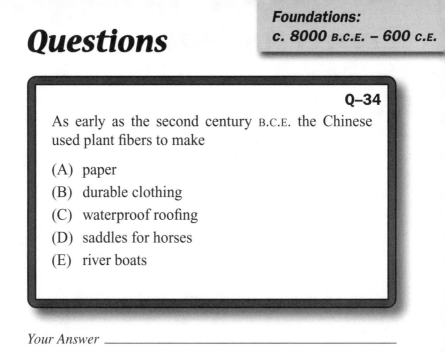

Q–34

As early as the second century B.C.E. the Chinese used plant fibers to make

(A) paper

(B) durable clothing

(C) waterproof roofing

(D) saddles for horses

(E) river boats

Your Answer _____

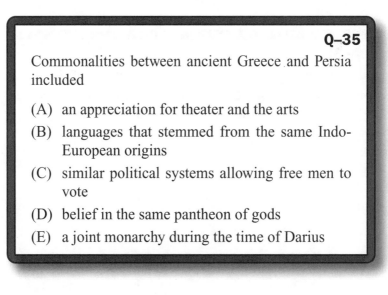

Q–35

Commonalities between ancient Greece and Persia included

(A) an appreciation for theater and the arts

(B) languages that stemmed from the same Indo-European origins

(C) similar political systems allowing free men to vote

(D) belief in the same pantheon of gods

(E) a joint monarchy during the time of Darius

Your Answer _____

Correct Answers

A–34

(A) Paper was an ancient Chinese innovation and was made from organic plant fibers soaked with bark and pounded with a mallet. It could then be formed into sheets and dried to make crude paper.

A–35

(B) Among some of the common features of Greek and Persian cultures were languages that belonged to the same Indo-European family of languages.

Questions

Q–36

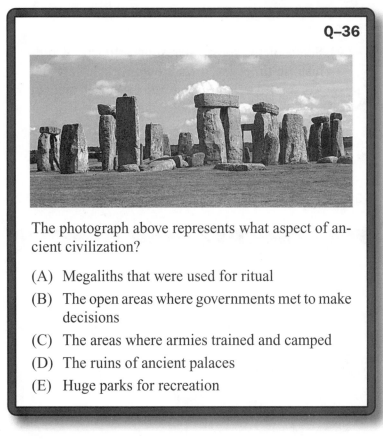

The photograph above represents what aspect of ancient civilization?

(A) Megaliths that were used for ritual

(B) The open areas where governments met to make decisions

(C) The areas where armies trained and camped

(D) The ruins of ancient palaces

(E) Huge parks for recreation

Your Answer _____

_____

Correct Answers

A–36

(A) Some of the most interesting artifacts of pre-historic times are great stone works of art and worship. The most famous is Stonehenge in England, which has been the subject of great speculation by historians through the centuries. These pre-Roman structures may have had religious significance or were an early type of astrological patterning.

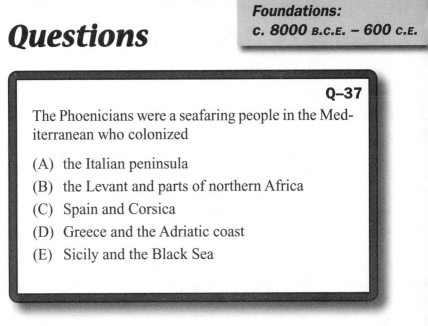

Q–37

The Phoenicians were a seafaring people in the Mediterranean who colonized

(A) the Italian peninsula
(B) the Levant and parts of northern Africa
(C) Spain and Corsica
(D) Greece and the Adriatic coast
(E) Sicily and the Black Sea

Your Answer _____

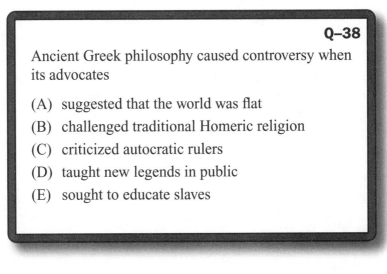

Q–38

Ancient Greek philosophy caused controversy when its advocates

(A) suggested that the world was flat
(B) challenged traditional Homeric religion
(C) criticized autocratic rulers
(D) taught new legends in public
(E) sought to educate slaves

Your Answer _____

Correct Answers

A–37

(B) The Phoenicians were associated earlier with the eastern Mediterranean area called Canaan. After 900 B.C.E., the Phoenicians established colonies on Cyprus and eventually the north-western coast of Africa. Eventually, their trade routes covered most of the Mediterranean.

A–38

(B) Pre-Socratic philosophers sometimes rejected popular myths about the origins of humankind and the world. They postulated different ideas about the material that made up the natural world and even questioned the anthropomorphic gods that were worshipped in the area.

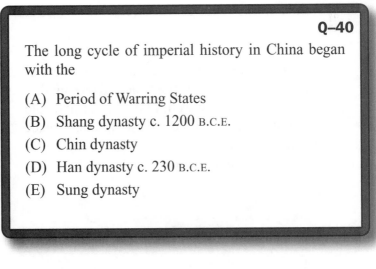

Q–39

A reason for the decline of the Roman republic was

(A) a series of powerful military leaders who destabilized the political order

(B) a famine that decimated the population

(C) the revolt in Gaul

(D) a passive urban population

(E) trade routes to North Africa being cut

Your Answer _____

Q–40

The long cycle of imperial history in China began with the

(A) Period of Warring States

(B) Shang dynasty c. 1200 B.C.E.

(C) Chin dynasty

(D) Han dynasty c. 230 B.C.E.

(E) Sung dynasty

Your Answer _____

Correct Answers

A–39

(A) After 88 B.C.E., a number of ambitious senator-warlords wanted to gain power. They took power unto themselves and undermined the old democratic order. In fighting one another, a series of civil wars led to the rise of a new series of dictator-emperors, starting with Julius Caesar.

A–40

(D) Historians mark the Han dynasty as the beginning of a tradition of political and cultural continuity for China. Dynasties followed one another in turn as a family would take power and rule until another group would rise up and replace them. Emperors ruled from a capital and divided territories into provinces.

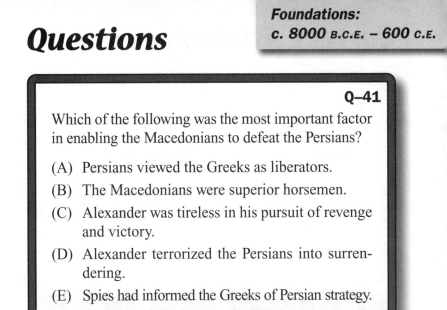

Q–41

Which of the following was the most important factor in enabling the Macedonians to defeat the Persians?

(A) Persians viewed the Greeks as liberators.

(B) The Macedonians were superior horsemen.

(C) Alexander was tireless in his pursuit of revenge and victory.

(D) Alexander terrorized the Persians into surrendering.

(E) Spies had informed the Greeks of Persian strategy.

Your Answer _____

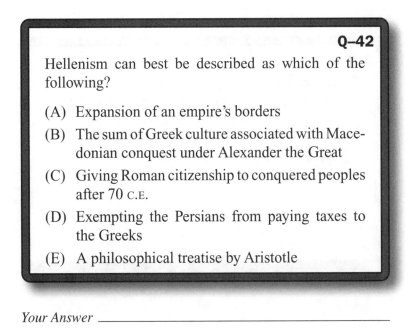

Q–42

Hellenism can best be described as which of the following?

(A) Expansion of an empire's borders

(B) The sum of Greek culture associated with Macedonian conquest under Alexander the Great

(C) Giving Roman citizenship to conquered peoples after 70 C.E.

(D) Exempting the Persians from paying taxes to the Greeks

(E) A philosophical treatise by Aristotle

Your Answer _____

Correct Answers

A–41

(C) Alexander wished to punish the Persians for the destruction of Athens in 480 B.C.E. and pursued Darius across the Middle East. After numerous victories, the Persians turned on Darius and killed him. Alexander was then able to take control of one of the most well-known ancient empires.

A–42

(B) Hellenism is the descriptor used for ancient Greek culture. From the Golden Age of Athens to the conquest of the world under Alexander, Greek culture was spread from the Aegean to India by the conquering Macedonians.

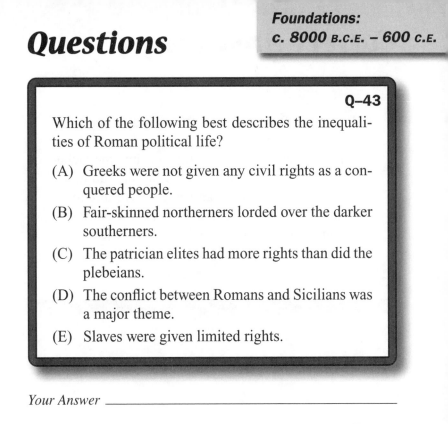

Q–43

Which of the following best describes the inequalities of Roman political life?

(A) Greeks were not given any civil rights as a conquered people.

(B) Fair-skinned northerners lorded over the darker southerners.

(C) The patrician elites had more rights than did the plebeians.

(D) The conflict between Romans and Sicilians was a major theme.

(E) Slaves were given limited rights.

Your Answer _____

_____

Correct Answers

A–43

(C) The Conflict of the Orders was a struggle between the patricians and the majority of the population, the plebeians. Over time the plebeians won more concessions from the ruling patricians. Some plebeian leaders were lured into an expanded elite class, and thus the patricians could hold on to some of their privileges.

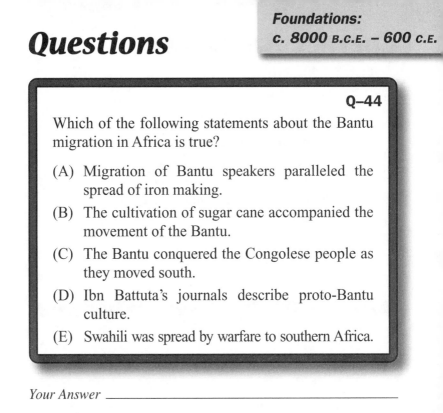

Q–44

Which of the following statements about the Bantu migration in Africa is true?

(A) Migration of Bantu speakers paralleled the spread of iron making.

(B) The cultivation of sugar cane accompanied the movement of the Bantu.

(C) The Bantu conquered the Congolese people as they moved south.

(D) Ibn Battuta's journals describe proto-Bantu culture.

(E) Swahili was spread by warfare to southern Africa.

Your Answer _____

_____

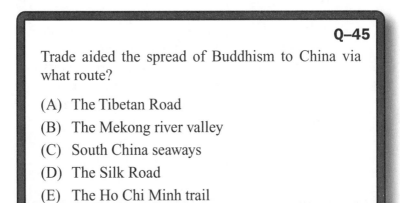

Q–45

Trade aided the spread of Buddhism to China via what route?

(A) The Tibetan Road

(B) The Mekong river valley

(C) South China seaways

(D) The Silk Road

(E) The Ho Chi Minh trail

Your Answer _____

_____

Correct Answers

A–44

(A) Some African languages can be traced to Bantu culture, which spread southward after the first millennium B.C.E. It is believed the Bantu originated in the area of present-day Nigeria and migrated south into sub-Saharan Africa over many generations.

A–45

(D) As an ancient trade route, the Silk Road was used as a means of spreading Buddhism by King Asoka from South Asia after the third century B.C.E. Asoka had sent out monks, missionaries, and pilgrims to promote the spread of the religion. These representatives helped spread the Buddhist faith to East and Southeast Asia by the second century C.E.

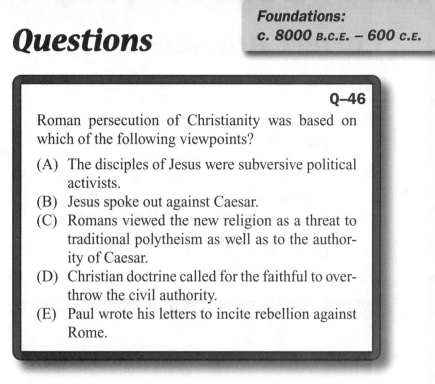

Q–46

Roman persecution of Christianity was based on which of the following viewpoints?

(A) The disciples of Jesus were subversive political activists.

(B) Jesus spoke out against Caesar.

(C) Romans viewed the new religion as a threat to traditional polytheism as well as to the authority of Caesar.

(D) Christian doctrine called for the faithful to overthrow the civil authority.

(E) Paul wrote his letters to incite rebellion against Rome.

Your Answer _____

_____

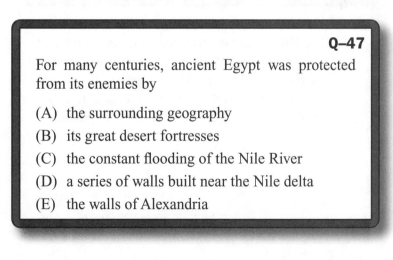

Q–47

For many centuries, ancient Egypt was protected from its enemies by

(A) the surrounding geography

(B) its great desert fortresses

(C) the constant flooding of the Nile River

(D) a series of walls built near the Nile delta

(E) the walls of Alexandria

Your Answer _____

_____

Correct Answers

A–46

(C) Rome was initially perplexed by the growing popularity of what was at first a sect of Judaism in Judea. As more people converted to Christianity, it came to be viewed as a dangerous cult focused on a Jewish rabbi. Persecution took many forms, from loss of rights to execution, but many Roman citizens were also converted by the second century C.E.

A–47

(A) The Nile region is protected by desert to the east and west. The Nile itself is hard to navigate to the south given the rapids as it descends from the Sudan. To the north is the Mediterranean, so invasion from there would have to be amphibious.

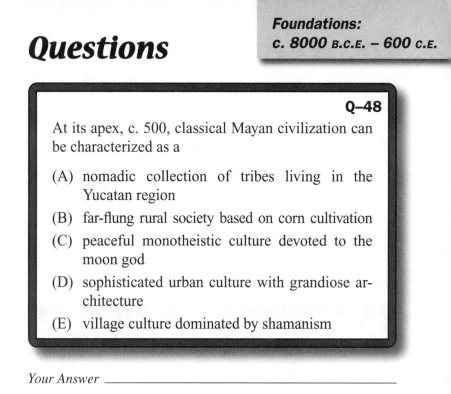

Q–48

At its apex, c. 500, classical Mayan civilization can be characterized as a

(A) nomadic collection of tribes living in the Yucatan region

(B) far-flung rural society based on corn cultivation

(C) peaceful monotheistic culture devoted to the moon god

(D) sophisticated urban culture with grandiose architecture

(E) village culture dominated by shamanism

Your Answer _____

_____

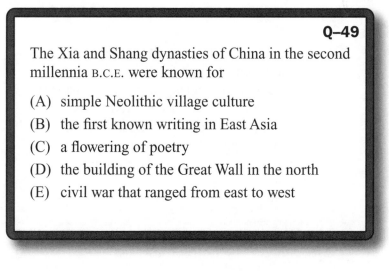

Q–49

The Xia and Shang dynasties of China in the second millennia B.C.E. were known for

(A) simple Neolithic village culture

(B) the first known writing in East Asia

(C) a flowering of poetry

(D) the building of the Great Wall in the north

(E) civil war that ranged from east to west

Your Answer _____

_____

Correct Answers

A–48

(D) Mayan civilization was discovered by archeologists and historians in the last century. Large cities such as Tikal on the Yucatan peninsula reveal an urban culture with sophisticated religious rituals that involved worship of numerous nature gods. The civilization declined rapidly after 900 C.E. for reasons that are still being debated.

A–49

(B) Few records of the earliest Chinese dynasties have survived. Around 2000 B.C.E., the earliest evidence of a written language begins to appear. The pictographic drawings evolved into symbols with meanings and pronunciations. Early materials such as bone and stone were used as surfaces that early Chinese would make records on.

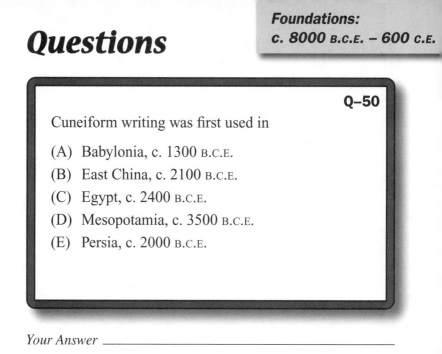

Q–50

Cuneiform writing was first used in

(A) Babylonia, c. 1300 B.C.E.

(B) East China, c. 2100 B.C.E.

(C) Egypt, c. 2400 B.C.E.

(D) Mesopotamia, c. 3500 B.C.E.

(E) Persia, c. 2000 B.C.E.

Your Answer _____

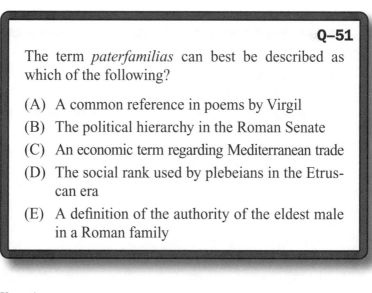

Q–51

The term *paterfamilias* can best be described as which of the following?

(A) A common reference in poems by Virgil

(B) The political hierarchy in the Roman Senate

(C) An economic term regarding Mediterranean trade

(D) The social rank used by plebeians in the Etrus-can era

(E) A definition of the authority of the eldest male in a Roman family

Your Answer _____

Correct Answers

A–50

(D) Writing is first traced to West Asia in the fourth millennia B.C.E. and was used to record business transactions. A reed was used to make wedge-shaped marks in clay. These tablets record early communication in the Tigris and Euphrates area.

A–51

(E) The father or eldest male had great authority over his family in ancient Rome. He had the final say in family matters, and the wife, slaves, and all children had to defer to him in most matters. This male-dominated order was a centerpiece of Roman culture.

Questions

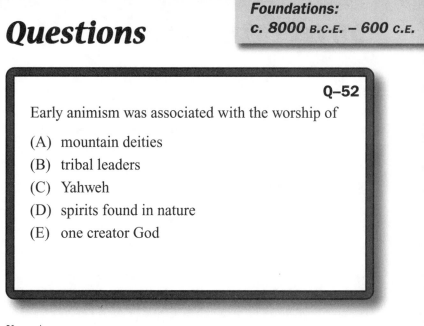

Q–52

Early animism was associated with the worship of

(A) mountain deities

(B) tribal leaders

(C) Yahweh

(D) spirits found in nature

(E) one creator God

Your Answer _____

_____

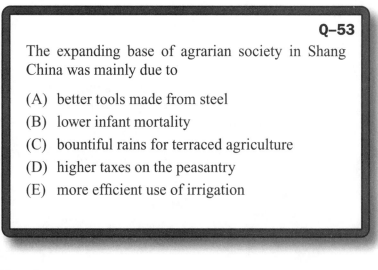

Q–53

The expanding base of agrarian society in Shang China was mainly due to

(A) better tools made from steel

(B) lower infant mortality

(C) bountiful rains for terraced agriculture

(D) higher taxes on the peasantry

(E) more efficient use of irrigation

Your Answer _____

_____

Correct Answers

A–52

(D) Ancient humans lived in close relationship with nature. Early civilization is characterized by the polytheistic and animistic worship of natural spirits. Rituals were developed that sought to appease the forces of their natural world.

A–53

(E) A key development to expanding sedentary farming was the ability to control water flow and access. Early Chinese farmers began to divert rivers into canals and used human-powered wheels to bring water to fields. The farther the distance from the source of water, the more ingenious the system of irrigation needed to be.

Q–54

The Byzantine empire prospered greatly in large part because of

(A) its geographical location

(B) its conquering of the Carthaginians

(C) an alliance with the Seljuks

(D) the lower taxes imposed by the emperor

(E) its rising population

Your Answer _____

Q–55

The kingdom of ancient Israel was ruled by

(A) the committee of the Twelve

(B) the priestly class

(C) a king anointed by a prophet

(D) a holy shaman

(E) a warrior class

Your Answer _____

Correct Answers

A–54

(A) The Byzantine empire lies at the crossroads between Europe and the rest of west Asia. The known ancient world could be accessed to the east and the west. The Black Sea also provided a gateway to the Rus, the predecessors of the Russians.

A–55

(C) The people of Israel were first led by Moses out of Egypt, after which a series of judges led the twelve tribes as they settled in Canaan. Later a larger kingdom was created, and a king was chosen by a prophet. The kingdom reached its greatest power under King David and then his son Solomon.

Questions

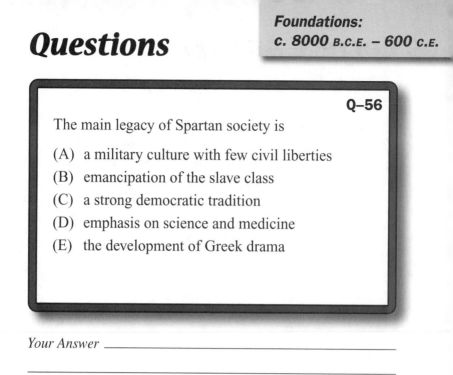

Q–56

The main legacy of Spartan society is

(A) a military culture with few civil liberties
(B) emancipation of the slave class
(C) a strong democratic tradition
(D) emphasis on science and medicine
(E) the development of Greek drama

Your Answer _____

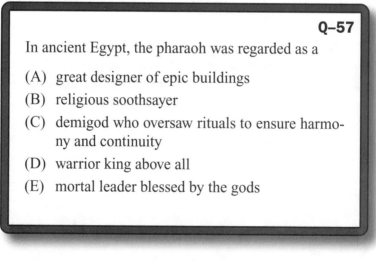

Q–57

In ancient Egypt, the pharaoh was regarded as a

(A) great designer of epic buildings
(B) religious soothsayer
(C) demigod who oversaw rituals to ensure harmony and continuity
(D) warrior king above all
(E) mortal leader blessed by the gods

Your Answer _____

Correct Answers

A–56

(A) Spartan society in ancient Greece was highly regimented and militaristic. Young men were trained from an early age to fight and die as citizens of their city-state. This fostered a collectivism that allowed for few personal liberties. It had a slave class; its members were called *helots* and they had no rights.

A–57

(C) Ancient Egypt was a quasi-theocracy with a pharaoh who was a monarch who also had religious duties. Many rituals centered on the animistic worship of the Nile River. The pharaoh was a divine personality who had special knowledge of the divine.

Q–58

A common feature of ancient Chinese rule was the

(A) federalistic approach to government
(B) use of forced labor to construct buildings and defensive barriers
(C) decentralized bureaucracy
(D) allowing of criticism by the scholar class
(E) alliance with Japanese warlords

Your Answer _____

Q–59

The earliest variant of the *Homo sapien* was the

(A) Kenya man
(B) Bronze age man
(C) Neanderthal man
(D) bipedal simian
(E) Cro-Magnon man

Your Answer _____

Correct Answers

A–58

(B) The first emperor Shi Huangdi set the pattern for rule in China by creating large public works projects such as the Great Wall to protect China on the northern frontier. Thousands of people were forced to work on these construction efforts. He also burned scholars who criticized him, thus showing the intolerance for dissent in imperial China.

A–59

(C) The Neanderthal man is traced back to a quarter million years ago. He wore clothing and created semipermanent dwellings.

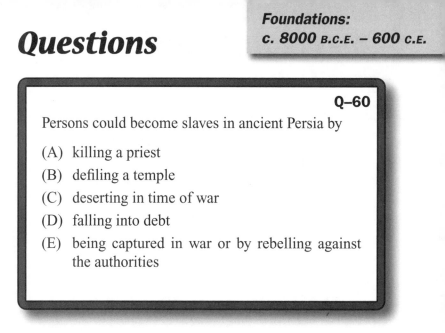

Q–60

Persons could become slaves in ancient Persia by

(A) killing a priest

(B) defiling a temple

(C) deserting in time of war

(D) falling into debt

(E) being captured in war or by rebelling against the authorities

Your Answer _____

_____

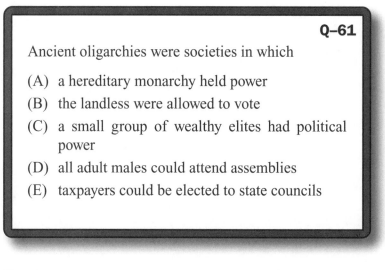

Q–61

Ancient oligarchies were societies in which

(A) a hereditary monarchy held power

(B) the landless were allowed to vote

(C) a small group of wealthy elites had political power

(D) all adult males could attend assemblies

(E) taxpayers could be elected to state councils

Your Answer _____

_____

Correct Answers

A–60

(E) Slaves were often the spoils of war, after which the Persian army would capture large numbers of the enemy and bring them back as booty. Slaves could also be political dissenters who were sold into slavery for opposing the imperial government. Slave status meant the loss of all personal freedom.

A–61

(C) An oligarchy, by definition, is the "rule of the few." This often meant the rich and powerful controlled the political system. Power and wealth were often a function of land ownership. In Rome, senators were often patricians with wealth and family connections who made up the elite of society.

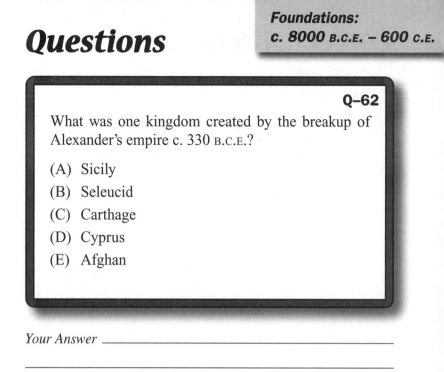

Q–62

What was one kingdom created by the breakup of Alexander's empire c. 330 B.C.E.?

(A) Sicily

(B) Seleucid

(C) Carthage

(D) Cyprus

(E) Afghan

Your Answer _____

_____

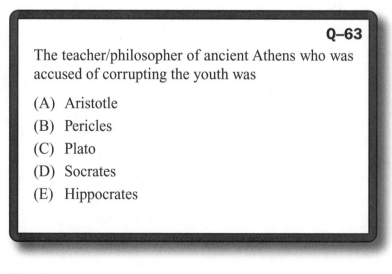

Q–63

The teacher/philosopher of ancient Athens who was accused of corrupting the youth was

(A) Aristotle

(B) Pericles

(C) Plato

(D) Socrates

(E) Hippocrates

Your Answer _____

_____

Correct Answers

A–62

(B) Alexander's empire was divided among his generals after his death in 330 B.C.E. Seleucis was given Syria and Persia as his domain, and he created a dynasty to rule it until the Romans conquered them in 80 B.C.E.

A–63

(D) In 399 B.C.E. Socrates was accused of teachings that were detrimental to the youth of the city of Athens. He was tried and sentenced to commit suicide. His trial is one of the most famous in history and highlights the difficulties in maintaining freedom of thought.

Q–64

After the death of Alexander the Great, India was united under the

(A) Augustine empire

(B) Gupta empire

(C) Maurya empire

(D) sultan of Persia

(E) Dalai Lama

Your Answer _____

Q–65

In Hinduism, to be released from the cycle of reincarnation is called

(A) divine escape

(B) maharesh

(C) yogi

(D) atman

(E) moksha

Your Answer _____

Correct Answers

A–64

(C) The Maurya empire filled the void that was left in India after the great Macedonian and Persian armies withdrew. After the death of Alexander, his appointed rulers were vulnerable to attack and Chandragupta led his armies to defeat the remaining provinces left from the Hellenistic empire.

A–65

(E) Hindus believe in the transmigration of the human soul, and one can be reborn as another living being after death. One goes through multiple existences and hopes to escape this rebirthing at some point in time. To rise to another spiritual plane without being reborn is called *moksha*.

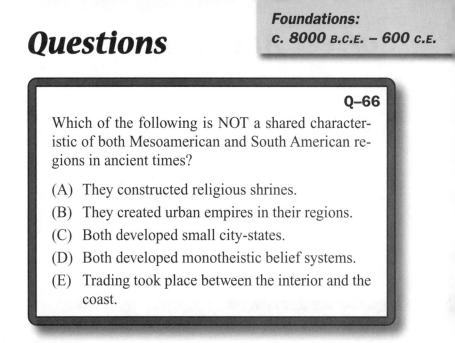

Q–66

Which of the following is NOT a shared characteristic of both Mesoamerican and South American regions in ancient times?

(A) They constructed religious shrines.

(B) They created urban empires in their regions.

(C) Both developed small city-states.

(D) Both developed monotheistic belief systems.

(E) Trading took place between the interior and the coast.

Your Answer _____

_____

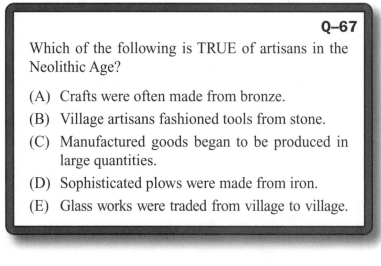

Q–67

Which of the following is TRUE of artisans in the Neolithic Age?

(A) Crafts were often made from bronze.

(B) Village artisans fashioned tools from stone.

(C) Manufactured goods began to be produced in large quantities.

(D) Sophisticated plows were made from iron.

(E) Glass works were traded from village to village.

Your Answer _____

_____

Correct Answers

A–66

(D) Both the Aztecs and the Incas established city-states and regional empires. Their religious practices were polytheistic, however, and it took the Spanish to introduce the idea of a single creator God.

A–67

(B) The Neolithic or New Stone Age, c. 8000 B.C.E., saw both the beginnings of prehistoric village life but also the use of stone materials for tools. Obsidian was a volcanic glassy rock found in nature and was used for sharp implements. Hunting and fishing became more efficient with the production of better tools and weapons.

Q–68

Artifacts used in early forms of nature worship were often represented by

(A) human and animal forms that suggested fertility
(B) mountain shapes
(C) deities made of bird feathers
(D) wooden boxes carved from cyprus
(E) bones with pictographs carved on them

Your Answer _____

Q–69

Which of the following is an accurate statement about early Roman land reform?

(A) Tribunes opposed the distribution of farmland to peasants.
(B) Opposition in the Senate led to violence and murder.
(C) Slaves were sometimes freed and given land by their masters.
(D) It resulted from the war with Carthage.
(E) Grain was taxed to pay for new lands.

Your Answer _____

Correct Answers

A–68

(A) Fertility is one of the most common themes of ancient idol worship. Fertility encompassed both the human desire for offspring and also the need for the land to yield crops for human consumption. Temple worship and other rituals could revolve around appeasing the gods of nature so that there would be enough food to eat.

A–69

(B) Tribunes were chosen to represent more of the people, and the tribunes were often in favor of giving land to the poorer classes. This met with strong resistance from older patricians, especially leaders in the Senate. Around 133 B.C.E., a tribune, Tiberius Sempronius, was murdered by conservative supporters of the Senate because he wanted to give land to poor soldiers as a reward for their service.

Q–70

Knowledge about the nomadic barbarians who invaded ancient Greece and Rome is limited because

(A) their language has been impossible to decode by scholars

(B) there is no mention of them by ancient historians

(C) they vanished mysteriously after 500 C.E.

(D) Christianity absorbed their culture after 350 C.E.

(E) they had no written language and left no records

Your Answer _____

_____

Q–71

Which of the following lands were NOT included in the Byzantine empire?

(A) Greece

(B) Asia Minor

(C) Syria

(D) Gaul

(E) Egypt

Your Answer _____

_____

Correct Answers

A–70

(E) Ancient peoples who had no written language are difficult to study. The only sources that describe them are from the peoples who contacted them, or vice versa. The Huns and Goths fought with the Romans and Greeks and are mentioned in their records. But the information is limited to military contacts, and less is known of their culture and way of life.

A–71

(D) After the collapse of the Western Roman Empire, the eastern part of the Roman empire became known as the Byzantine empire. It included parts of North Africa, the Balkans, and the Middle East. Gaul (present-day France), however, was part of the western empire and not part of Byzantium.

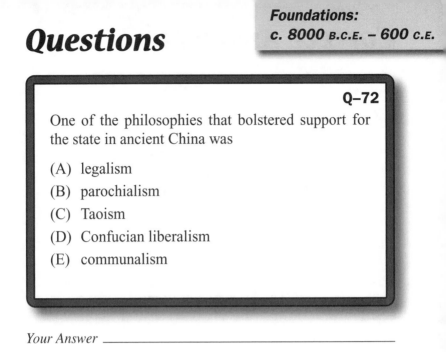

Q–72

One of the philosophies that bolstered support for the state in ancient China was

(A) legalism
(B) parochialism
(C) Taoism
(D) Confucian liberalism
(E) communalism

Your Answer _____

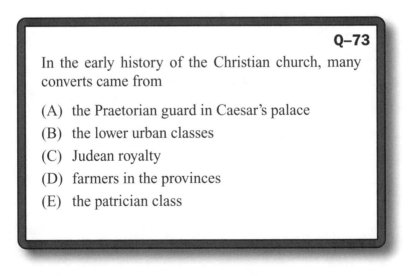

Q–73

In the early history of the Christian church, many converts came from

(A) the Praetorian guard in Caesar's palace
(B) the lower urban classes
(C) Judean royalty
(D) farmers in the provinces
(E) the patrician class

Your Answer _____

Correct Answers

A–72

(A) Legalism grew out of the Hundred Schools of Thought that followed the chaos of the Warring States period. It promoted strict laws and obedience to the state and gave great power to the ruler. It is an early totalitarian school of political thought that allowed for abuses by the authorities.

A–73

(B) The teachings of Jesus of Nazareth were more attractive to the poorer city dwellers, who found comfort in a personal God that did not differentiate between peoples. Equality of the sexes and respect for slaves were radical new ideas that Christianity espoused.

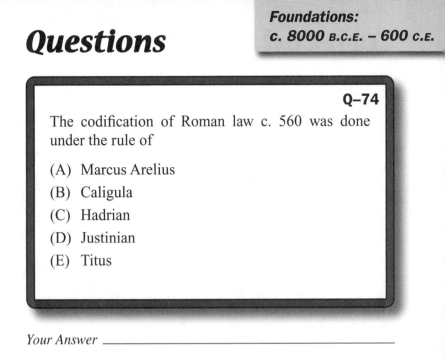

Q–74

The codification of Roman law c. 560 was done under the rule of

(A) Marcus Arelius

(B) Caligula

(C) Hadrian

(D) Justinian

(E) Titus

Your Answer _____

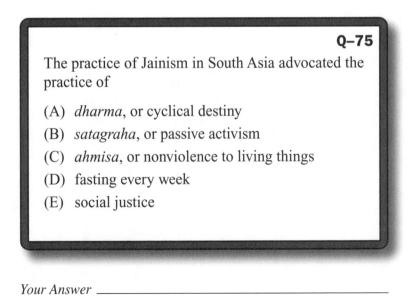

Q–75

The practice of Jainism in South Asia advocated the practice of

(A) *dharma*, or cyclical destiny

(B) *satagraha*, or passive activism

(C) *ahmisa*, or nonviolence to living things

(D) fasting every week

(E) social justice

Your Answer _____

Correct Answers

A–74

(D) In the early Byzantine empire, the emperor Justinian called for a comprehensive review of Roman law. From this review, he distilled the legal principles of ancient Rome and codified it for his use as ruler of Byzantium.

A–75

(C) In India, a religious teacher named Vardhamana Mahavira preached comprehensive nonviolence and respect for all living things. Devout followers would even brush the ground in front of them as they walked to avoid stepping on insects. Jainism stressed that all creatures are sacred, so they have a strict diet of only organic plants.

Q–76

Which of the following was a natural resource that was central to southern Saharan trade in ancient times?

(A) Palm oil

(B) Dates

(C) Salt

(D) Fur

(E) Copper

Your Answer _____

_____

Q–77

The Silk Road encouraged the spread of which of the following military technologies?

(A) Mounted bowmen and the stirrup

(B) Trebuchets and spears

(C) Greek fire and the phalanx

(D) The curved sword and the shield

(E) Bronze helmets and gunpowder

Your Answer _____

_____

Correct Answers

A–76

(C) Salt was a crucial commodity in the Saharan desert frontier to the south. Cut into slabs, it was a valuable item in African trade beginning around 300. In the hot desert environment, salt was vital for survival.

A–77

(A) Men on horseback with bows were a Mongol innovation that was used to devastating effect by the khan and his armies. The Silk Road, as an established trade route, also served as a route for conquering armies after 1230. The use of the stirrup to keep the rider in his saddle was also seen along the Silk Road as the Mongol armies spread west.

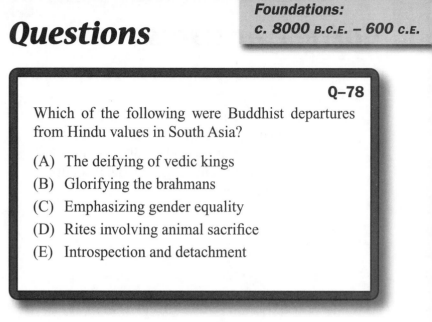

Q–78

Which of the following were Buddhist departures from Hindu values in South Asia?

(A) The deifying of vedic kings

(B) Glorifying the brahmans

(C) Emphasizing gender equality

(D) Rites involving animal sacrifice

(E) Introspection and detachment

Your Answer _____

_____

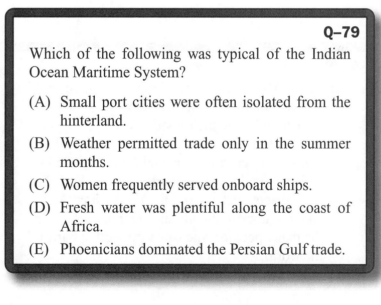

Q–79

Which of the following was typical of the Indian Ocean Maritime System?

(A) Small port cities were often isolated from the hinterland.

(B) Weather permitted trade only in the summer months.

(C) Women frequently served onboard ships.

(D) Fresh water was plentiful along the coast of Africa.

(E) Phoenicians dominated the Persian Gulf trade.

Your Answer _____

_____

Correct Answers

A–78

(E) Buddhism differed because it did not have a pantheon of epic gods like Hinduism did. It also preached detachment and meditative, personal introspection that challenged the fatalism of the Hindu worldview.

A–79

(A) In the Middle East and along the east coast of Africa, small port cities developed for ships to stop at and trade their goods. Often poorly supplied with water, these small cities were isolated from the interior of Asia and Africa by climate and geography. Island ports such as Zanzibar were disconnected from the rest of East Africa and became multicultural communities, given the many peoples who came from other parts of the world.

Q–80

What instrument is a common cultural characteristic of ancient African music?

(A) The brass horn
(B) The flute
(C) The mandolin
(D) The drum
(E) The lyre

Your Answer _____

_____

600 – 1450

Q–81

The Mongols and the Ottomans both had what kind of political leadership?

(A) Quasi-democratic parliaments
(B) Autocratic governance
(C) A constitutional monarchy
(D) A confederation of warlords
(E) Single-party dictators

Your Answer _____

_____

Correct Answers

A–80

(D) Different groups in Africa played various instruments in their celebrations and tribal rituals. The drum was widely used as a basic rhythmic centerpiece of African experience. This gave African music a distinctive percussive character that is observable throughout the continent.

A–81

(B) Both the Ottomans and Mongols ruled autocratically, whether through the sultan in Constantinople or the khan in Khanbalik (present-day Beijing). Decisions were made from the thrones of these powerful rulers and were carried out in the provinces.

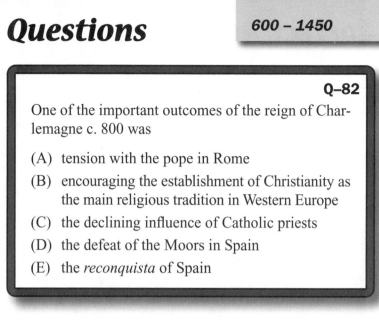

Q–82

One of the important outcomes of the reign of Charlemagne c. 800 was

(A) tension with the pope in Rome

(B) encouraging the establishment of Christianity as the main religious tradition in Western Europe

(C) the declining influence of Catholic priests

(D) the defeat of the Moors in Spain

(E) the *reconquista* of Spain

Your Answer _____

_____

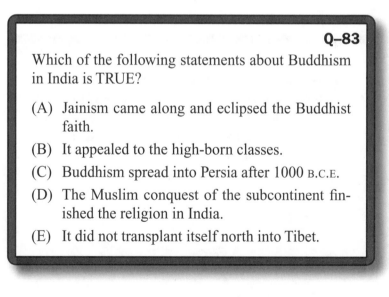

Q–83

Which of the following statements about Buddhism in India is TRUE?

(A) Jainism came along and eclipsed the Buddhist faith.

(B) It appealed to the high-born classes.

(C) Buddhism spread into Persia after 1000 B.C.E.

(D) The Muslim conquest of the subcontinent finished the religion in India.

(E) It did not transplant itself north into Tibet.

Your Answer _____

_____

Correct Answers

A–82

(B) Charlemagne was the most prominent Christian monarch of the early medieval period in Europe. The Frankish king helped establish the Christian church and its traditions in the area now known as France and Germany.

A–83

(D) Buddhism was born out of the early Hindu culture of India. It differed enough from Hinduism to create tensions between the two belief systems. When the Islamic faith spread into the subcontinent, it helped diminish the following of the religion.

Q–84

Early conflict and fighting resulted in Arabia after Mohammed began preaching his new faith and when Islam challenged the

(A) Berber ruling class in North Africa
(B) Egyptian practice of nepotism in government
(C) polygamous customs of the urban classes
(D) tribal polytheism of Arab culture
(E) trading laws in Arabia

Your Answer _____

_____

Q–85

Mohammed referred to his new belief system as *Islam,* meaning

(A) "God rules"
(B) "submission to God"
(C) "the faith of Allah"
(D) "People of the Book"
(E) "Blessed Revelation"

Your Answer _____

_____

Correct Answers

A–84

(D) Mohammed was born into the commercial culture of Mecca in 570 Mecca was a caravan city where trade and religious ritual were the main businesses. Multiple gods were worshipped in Mecca by travelers as they passed through. When Mohammed began to preach of a single exclusive God, it threatened the customs and orthodoxy of this town. The early followers of Islam were attacked and then expelled from their home, and the survivors sought sanctuary in Medina.

A–85

(B) As a prophet, Mohammed proclaimed his new revelation and he called on people to submit to the creator God (Allah). Once this happened, the new convert was called a muslim, or one who has surrendered to the will of God.

Questions

Q–86

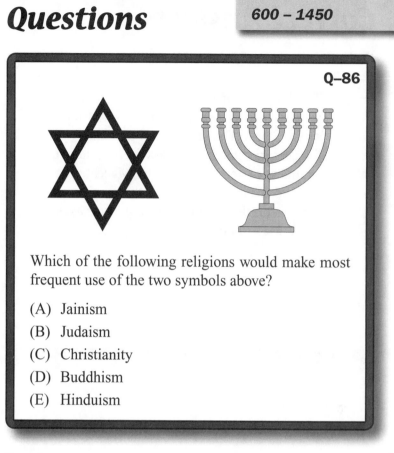

Which of the following religions would make most frequent use of the two symbols above?

(A) Jainism
(B) Judaism
(C) Christianity
(D) Buddhism
(E) Hinduism

Your Answer _____

Correct Answers

A–86

(B) The kingship of David c. 1000 B.C.E. has been remembered as the high-water mark of Judaism, so the Star of David has been used as a symbol for centuries by Jews. Likewise, the heroic reconquest of Jerusalem by the Maccabeens under Judah has given rise to the symbol of the candles on the Menorah. Jewish art makes frequent use of both symbols.

Questions

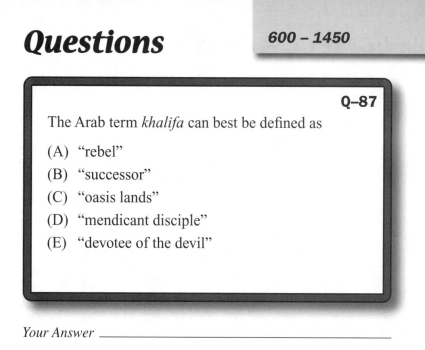

Q–87

The Arab term *khalifa* can best be defined as

(A) "rebel"
(B) "successor"
(C) "oasis lands"
(D) "mendicant disciple"
(E) "devotee of the devil"

Your Answer _____

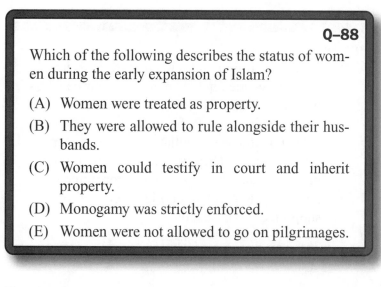

Q–88

Which of the following describes the status of women during the early expansion of Islam?

(A) Women were treated as property.
(B) They were allowed to rule alongside their husbands.
(C) Women could testify in court and inherit property.
(D) Monogamy was strictly enforced.
(E) Women were not allowed to go on pilgrimages.

Your Answer _____

Correct Answers

A–87

(B) After the death of Mohammed in 632, Muslim leaders chose Abu Bakr as the caliph, or successor of the prophet. This started a short line of Islamic rulers who took on the mantle of patriarchal leaders in early Islamic history. With the rapid spread of the religion through the Middle East, these immediate successors of Mohammed had to oversee the administration of new domains and peoples.

A–88

(C) Islamic tradition and law allowed considerable rights to women in the context of their day. Unlike women in other religions, Muslim women could retain property from the estate of a dead husband and even initiate divorce in certain circumstances. They were allowed to go on pilgrimages, and the first wife of Mohammed was revered as a moral and upright personality who supported her husband.

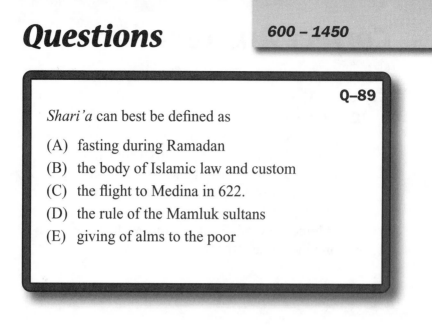

Q–89

Shari'a can best be defined as

(A) fasting during Ramadan

(B) the body of Islamic law and custom

(C) the flight to Medina in 622.

(D) the rule of the Mamluk sultans

(E) giving of alms to the poor

Your Answer _____

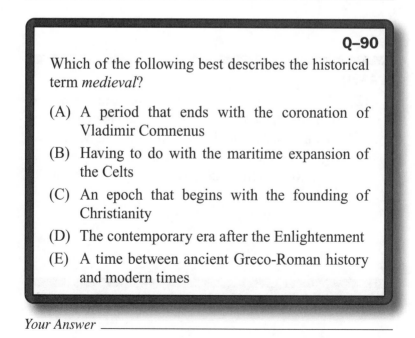

Q–90

Which of the following best describes the historical term *medieval*?

(A) A period that ends with the coronation of Vladimir Comnenus

(B) Having to do with the maritime expansion of the Celts

(C) An epoch that begins with the founding of Christianity

(D) The contemporary era after the Enlightenment

(E) A time between ancient Greco-Roman history and modern times

Your Answer _____

Correct Answers

A–89

(B) Islamic religious custom and law evolved over generations as Islam spread across the Middle East and North Africa. Codifying customs and also punishments was the work of Islamic scholars, who looked for authoritative roots for the oldest practices. Islamic rulers were expected to enforce the *sharia* as they oversaw the cities and provinces under them.

A–90

(E) Modern historians have looked back at the period after the collapse of Rome and labeled it as *medieval*, or belonging to the so-called Middle Ages. They have seen it as an interim period prior to modern times, which began with the Renaissance.

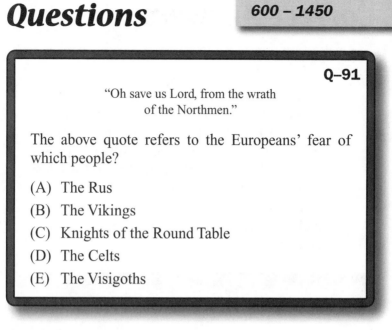

Q–91

"Oh save us Lord, from the wrath
of the Northmen."

The above quote refers to the Europeans' fear of which people?

(A) The Rus

(B) The Vikings

(C) Knights of the Round Table

(D) The Celts

(E) The Visigoths

Your Answer _____

_____

Correct Answers

A–91

(B) Near the end of the eighth century, raiding bands of Vikings, or Norsemen, began to attack the British Isles and parts of northern continental Europe. Using their longboats to strike quickly and brutally, the so-called Northmen struck fear in the inhabitants of kingdoms and monasteries across the continent. Their maritime skill and their aggressive military tactics were a potent combination.

Questions

Q–92

The picture above shows a building that is representative of _____ architecture.

(A) gothic

(B) baroque

(C) neoclassical

(D) art deco

(E) neo-modern

Your Answer _____

_____

Correct Answers

A–92

(A) Gothic architecture became a feature of medieval design in the 1100s in western Europe. It used rectangular shapes for the interior and pointed arches to create space. The ribbed vaults also give the space a vertical thrust. Famous gothic churches were erected in France, Germany, and England during the Middle Ages before the Renaissance emphasized other forms after 1400. Sandstone and limestone were used to create these large structures that stand today as monuments of Medieval engineering.

Questions

Q–93

The term *vassal* means

(A) a landless peasant
(B) the center of a fiefdom
(C) a status of mutual obligation between lord and underling
(D) a container for fluids
(E) clergy during medieval times

Your Answer _____

Q–94

Early Russia grew out of a principality centered in the city of

(A) Minsk
(B) Kiev
(C) St. Petersburg
(D) Novgorod
(E) Cracow

Your Answer _____

Correct Answers

A-93

(C) In the Middle Ages, power relationships were based on obligations of mutual military protection and service. A lord would have vassals oversee pieces of land in return for military service when defense of the realm was needed. Vassals would also have others help them work their portions of land and fight for them when necessary.

A-94

(B) Kievan Russia was established by Vladimir I when he and an army of Varangians retook Kiev and he became the grand prince. In converting to Orthodox Christianity, the inhabitants of Kiev expanded the eastern faith throughout the realm until the arrival of the Mongols.

Q–95

The population of western Europe nearly doubled from 1000 to 1200 because of the

(A) new farming technology, such as the improved plow and horse collar

(B) influx of Aryan peoples

(C) use of the potato as a foodstuff

(D) volcanic eruptions that enriched the soil

(E) relative peace that existed

Your Answer

Q–96

The decentralization of Islam took place after 1000 when

(A) Mohammed passed his authority on to his sons

(B) Shiite leaders broke away from the Abbasids

(C) the Turks took over Byzantium

(D) rival caliphates took power in North Africa and Spain

(E) Christianity took back portions of Syria during the Crusades

Your Answer

Correct Answers

A–95

(A) The use of improved plowing technology and wider use of horses for farm work allowed greater yields in medieval agriculture. Horses are faster than oxen, and the new collar transferred the pressure from the neck to the shoulders so that more power was generated. Soil that had been too heavy to work now was planted, and the increase in food production spurred the growth in population.

A–96

(D) Islam matured and diversified as it expanded. New interpretations of the faith and the inevitable waning of the centralized caliphates all helped the religion to fragment theologically and politically. New centers of power like that in Cordoba, Spain, competed with the older regimes in Baghdad so that the centrality of the old system weakened.

Questions

Q–97

Which of the following helped inspire the Crusades to recapture the Holy Land from Muslim forces?

(A) European rulers welcomed papal permission to fight non-Christians.

(B) Ambitious lords were eager to conquer new territories beyond Europe.

(C) Italian merchants wanted to have more access to Arab goods.

(D) The pope wanted to demonstrate political authority over kings and lords.

(E) All of the above

Your Answer _____

_____

Q–98

Differences between the Latin and Greek divisions within Christianity were widened when

(A) Constantinople was sacked by the Crusaders

(B) Islamic conquests in the Middle East cut Rome off from eastern Christendom

(C) Saladin retook Jerusalem

(D) editions of the Vulgate Bible became scarce

(E) the pope relocated to Avignon

Your Answer _____

_____

Correct Answers

A–97

(E) The complex power structure of medieval Europe revealed early tensions between feudal lords and the central power of Latin Christianity. When the pope called for the retaking of the holy city of Jerusalem from the Muslims, it released some of the tensions within medieval Europe. Some of these were economic and others were political. The encroachment of Islam in the southwest and southeast had also inspired a defensive reaction that called for a more unified response from Christendom.

A–98

(B) Communication within Christendom was affected when Syria, Egypt, and other areas came under the influence of Islam after the seventh century. This encouraged religious customs to diverge between eastern and western Europe. After this, political power emanated to the north of Rome as powerful kings and emperors established themselves in present-day France and Germany.

Q–99

The spread of Buddhism in China c. 800 was sponsored by

(A) Tibetan monks who traveled widely throughout East Asia

(B) Tang rulers who brought in missionaries from India

(C) the Han emperor Wei Ping

(D) Mongol scholars who came from the north

(E) Uighur tribesmen from the West

Your Answer _____

_____

Correct Answers

A–99

(B) Tang rulers found that Buddhism had some political applications that were beneficial. Some Buddhist theology suggested that the ruling class was granted a spiritual function in creating a harmonious society. A kind of synthesis of homegrown animism and Buddhist ideas gave rise to a belief in benevolent spirits that could help a king or emperor rule his people. Mahayana Buddhism seemed to allow the inclusion of local gods into its belief system, which encouraged the conversion of many Chinese.

Take Test-Readiness Quiz 1 on CD
(to review questions 1–99)

Q–100

The beacons are always alight, fighting
and marching never stop . . . .

Know therefore that the sword is
a cursed thing.

Li Po, Tang Poet, c. 750

The above Chinese poem speaks of the time period as one of

(A) rivalry with the Byzantine empire

(B) cultural borrowing from Korea

(C) a series of wars with competitor states

(D) literary emphasis on imperial matters

(E) peace with surrounding kingdoms

Your Answer _____

_____

Correct Answers

A–100

(C) The Tang dynasty reached its height around 750, when rival states were established to the west and southwest by the Uighurs and Tibetans. Warfare resulted for many years, which inspired historians and poets to lament the death and energy wasted in those campaigns. Tang and Tibetan power eventually waned, resulting in some political and military fragmentation.

Questions

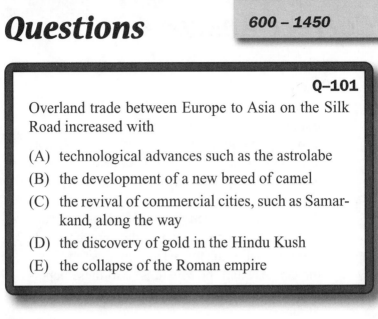

Q–101

Overland trade between Europe to Asia on the Silk Road increased with

(A) technological advances such as the astrolabe

(B) the development of a new breed of camel

(C) the revival of commercial cities, such as Samarkand, along the way

(D) the discovery of gold in the Hindu Kush

(E) the collapse of the Roman empire

Your Answer _____

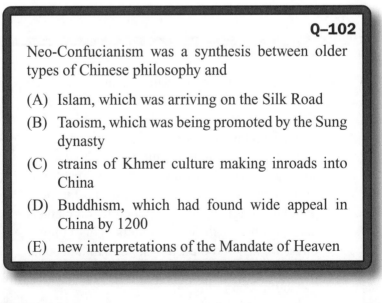

Q–102

Neo-Confucianism was a synthesis between older types of Chinese philosophy and

(A) Islam, which was arriving on the Silk Road

(B) Taoism, which was being promoted by the Sung dynasty

(C) strains of Khmer culture making inroads into China

(D) Buddhism, which had found wide appeal in China by 1200

(E) new interpretations of the Mandate of Heaven

Your Answer _____

Correct Answers

A–101

(C) Centers of commerce, such as Nishipur and Samarkand, grew and created more places for goods to be bought and sold. Traders could start with food such as dates and later deal in carpets and crafts along the Silk Road. A thriving proto-capitalistic system began to develop because the Abbasids encouraged the use of letters of credit. These were pieces of paper that proved funds were available to buy what was desired. Both the Chinese and the Muslims used these paper-based banking methods before the West learned of them.

A–102

(D) Neo-Confucianism is an interesting mix of the older traditional Chinese values and the newer beliefs that Buddhism brought to China after 1000. Buddhism was a foreign religion, but it addressed basic human questions about one's soul and eternal destiny. In combining traditional Chinese codes of behavior and the new, popular religious import, neo-Confucianists made room for different beliefs. This cultural diffusion allowed the Chinese to maintain some values and make room for others introduced by the south Asian religion.

Q–103

Japanese people can trace their roots to

(A) Okinawan migrants who sailed across the South China Sea

(B) Mongoloid peoples who crossed over the sea from mainland Asia

(C) Hawaiian sailors who came west across the Pacific

(D) Chinese immigrants who arrived over 3000 years ago

(E) Siberian nomads who came to the islands around 2400 B.C.E.

Your Answer _____

Q–104

The classical era of Japan took place during the _____ period.

(A) Heian

(B) Tokugawa

(C) Minamoto

(D) Meiji

(E) Fukugawa

Your Answer _____

Correct Answers

A–103

(B) The Japanese, or Yamato people, are believed to have crossed from the Korean peninsula to the islands of Japan over 4000 years ago. They are a Mongoloid stock with a language more related to Northeast Asia than China proper. They evolved from tribes who intermarried over time and held to their own animistic beliefs that came to be known as Shinto.

A–104

(A) Classical Japan is defined by the Heian era from 794 to 1119. This period of general peace and political stability allowed the arts to flourish and a more uniquely Japanese culture to take shape. Already influenced by Chinese ideas from abroad, the Heian period saw the court life of the dynasty develop along uniquely Japanese lines. Japanese written language became standardized, and the Japanese developed their own literary tradition.

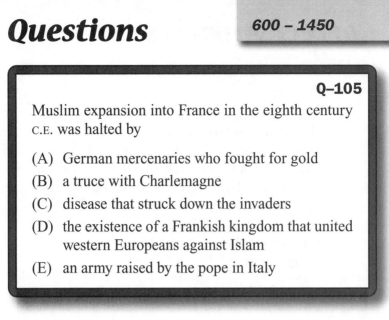

Q–105

Muslim expansion into France in the eighth century C.E. was halted by

(A) German mercenaries who fought for gold
(B) a truce with Charlemagne
(C) disease that struck down the invaders
(D) the existence of a Frankish kingdom that united western Europeans against Islam
(E) an army raised by the pope in Italy

Your Answer _____

_____

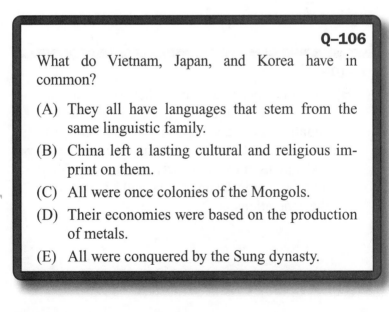

Q–106

What do Vietnam, Japan, and Korea have in common?

(A) They all have languages that stem from the same linguistic family.
(B) China left a lasting cultural and religious imprint on them.
(C) All were once colonies of the Mongols.
(D) Their economies were based on the production of metals.
(E) All were conquered by the Sung dynasty.

Your Answer _____

_____

Correct Answers

A–105

(D) After the conquest of Spain under the Muslims, Muslim northward expansion was stopped at the battle of Tours in 732. Under the leadership of Abd ar-Rahman, the Muslims met an army under Charles Martel, also known as the Hammer, in west central France. After a fierce battle, Rahman was killed and his Islamic army retreated over the mountains, never to threaten western Europe again.

A–106

(B) China has been the cultural heart of East Asia, and Chinese culture influenced surrounding countries in many ways. Buddhism spread to the south and east from China as missionaries and monks traveled widely. Confucian values all took root in Japan, Korea, and Vietnam over the generations.

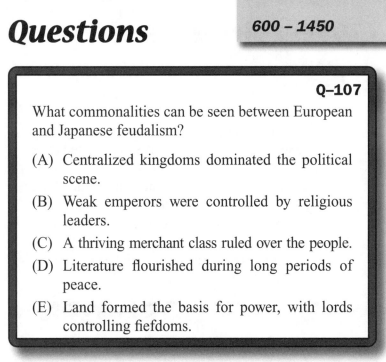

Q–107

What commonalities can be seen between European and Japanese feudalism?

(A) Centralized kingdoms dominated the political scene.

(B) Weak emperors were controlled by religious leaders.

(C) A thriving merchant class ruled over the people.

(D) Literature flourished during long periods of peace.

(E) Land formed the basis for power, with lords controlling fiefdoms.

Your Answer _____

_____

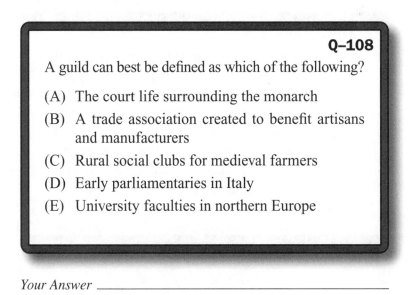

Q–108

A guild can best be defined as which of the following?

(A) The court life surrounding the monarch

(B) A trade association created to benefit artisans and manufacturers

(C) Rural social clubs for medieval farmers

(D) Early parliamentaries in Italy

(E) University faculties in northern Europe

Your Answer _____

_____

Correct Answers

A–107

(E) In both Europe and Japan, land was the key to wealth and power. Land and its produce could be taxed and controlled if lords maintained their small economies and formed alliances with other lords. Trade grew over time, but the merchant class was slow to gain influence. Small- and large-scale warfare was common, and powerful lords could gain power by holding sway over their territories with armies and vassals who fought for them.

A–108

(B) Business activity expanded in cities during the Middle Ages. One innovation to help organize early manufacture and artisanship was the creation of organizations called guilds. They regulated wages and prices that certain occupations could charge. They also codified the work of an apprentice who wanted to learn a trade and how apprentices would enter the workforce on their own after their training.

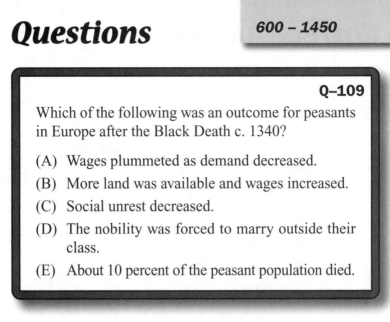

Q–109

Which of the following was an outcome for peasants in Europe after the Black Death c. 1340?

(A) Wages plummeted as demand decreased.

(B) More land was available and wages increased.

(C) Social unrest decreased.

(D) The nobility was forced to marry outside their class.

(E) About 10 percent of the peasant population died.

Your Answer _____

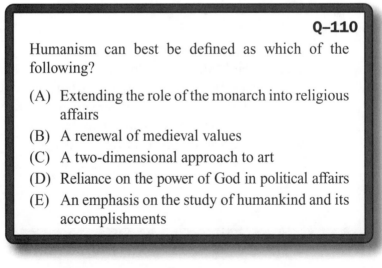

Q–110

Humanism can best be defined as which of the following?

(A) Extending the role of the monarch into religious affairs

(B) A renewal of medieval values

(C) A two-dimensional approach to art

(D) Reliance on the power of God in political affairs

(E) An emphasis on the study of humankind and its accomplishments

Your Answer _____

Correct Answers

A–109

(B) The devastation of the plague that spread from Asia to Europe in the fourteenth century had interesting economic and social effects on the peasantry of the time. Those who survived found abandoned tracts of land and a greater demand for their work. This caused greater mobility for the lower classes and encouraged them to demand more from the power elites. Urban revolts became more prevalent as a result.

A–110

(E) The Renaissance shifted from the religious themes of the Middle Ages to a more human-centered focus. While believing in God, humanists asserted the power of the individual and what the individual could create. This led to a flowering of art and science in Italy under geniuses such as Da Vinci and Michelangelo.

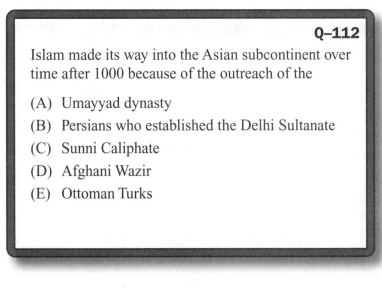

Q–111

Which of the following was the most unifying and monolithic institution in medieval Europe?

(A) The Holy Roman monarchy

(B) The artist's guild in urban areas

(C) The Roman Catholic Church

(D) The electors of Germany

(E) The Carolingian dynasty

Your Answer _____

_____

Q–112

Islam made its way into the Asian subcontinent over time after 1000 because of the outreach of the

(A) Umayyad dynasty

(B) Persians who established the Delhi Sultanate

(C) Sunni Caliphate

(D) Afghani Wazir

(E) Ottoman Turks

Your Answer _____

_____

Correct Answers

A–111

(C) The Roman Catholic Church gave Europe a common faith and hierarchy during the Middle Ages. While kings contended with popes at different times, the authority of the church was unassailable and all believers interacted with the Roman church throughout their lives. The pope had considerable influence in appointing powerful churchmen and also in allowing kings and princes to marry the right mates. Thus, religion and politics overlapped in complex ways.

A–112

(B) The Muslim religion and its political entities gradually conquered the Indian subcontinent by 1200. Also called the slave dynasty in its early period, the Delhi Sultanate was a succession of Muslim rulers who ruled northern India beginning in the thirteenth century.

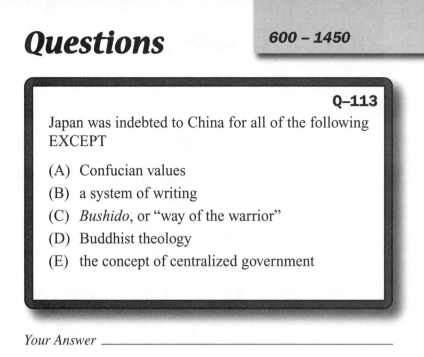

Q–113

Japan was indebted to China for all of the following EXCEPT

(A) Confucian values

(B) a system of writing

(C) *Bushido*, or "way of the warrior"

(D) Buddhist theology

(E) the concept of centralized government

Your Answer _____

_____

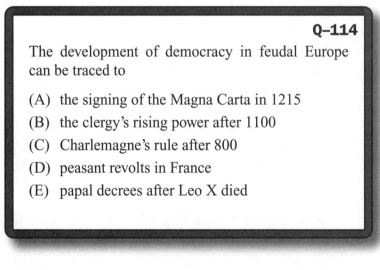

Q–114

The development of democracy in feudal Europe can be traced to

(A) the signing of the Magna Carta in 1215

(B) the clergy's rising power after 1100

(C) Charlemagne's rule after 800

(D) peasant revolts in France

(E) papal decrees after Leo X died

Your Answer _____

_____

Correct Answers

A–113

(C) The *Bushido*, or way of the warrior, is a uniquely Japanese tradition that defined samurai culture and values. The warrior class dominated feudal Japan, and its belief in honor and loyalty defined many interactions in its history. China did influence Japan profoundly in many cultural aspects such as religion, art, and political systems.

A–114

(A) When a handful of landed barons forced King John to sign the Magna Carta in 1215, a kind of shared power began to limit the power of the king. This led to a council of lords who advised the king and kept some of his power in check. The House of Lords allowed the aristocracy to become a feature of the government over the centuries.

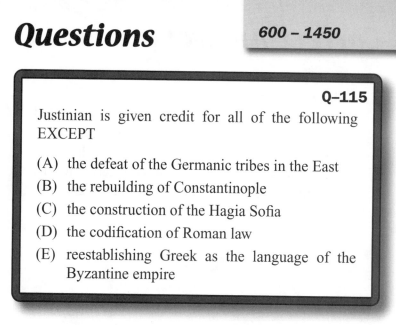

Q–115

Justinian is given credit for all of the following EXCEPT

(A) the defeat of the Germanic tribes in the East

(B) the rebuilding of Constantinople

(C) the construction of the Hagia Sofia

(D) the codification of Roman law

(E) reestablishing Greek as the language of the Byzantine empire

Your Answer _____

_____

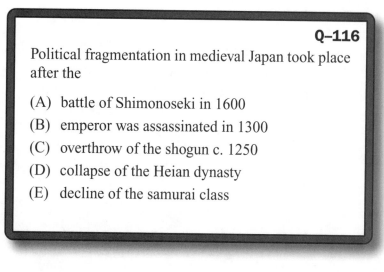

Q–116

Political fragmentation in medieval Japan took place after the

(A) battle of Shimonoseki in 1600

(B) emperor was assassinated in 1300

(C) overthrow of the shogun c. 1250

(D) collapse of the Heian dynasty

(E) decline of the samurai class

Your Answer _____

_____

Correct Answers

A–115

(E) Justinian knew that his empire was essentially Greek, and while Latin was the language of the government, he did not force its use in daily life. He was more famous for conquering Rome again and systematizing the Roman legal system in Byzantium and beyond.

A–116

(D) The collapse of Heian rule in Japan encouraged a descent into decentralization after 1179. The warrior class was gathered by different feudal lords into small armies and domains. The emperor remained in Kyoto but had less and less influence on political affairs as feudal lords staked their claims to different parts of the archipelago.

Questions

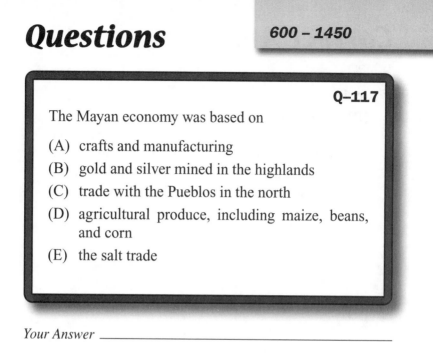

Q–117

The Mayan economy was based on

(A) crafts and manufacturing

(B) gold and silver mined in the highlands

(C) trade with the Pueblos in the north

(D) agricultural produce, including maize, beans, and corn

(E) the salt trade

Your Answer _____

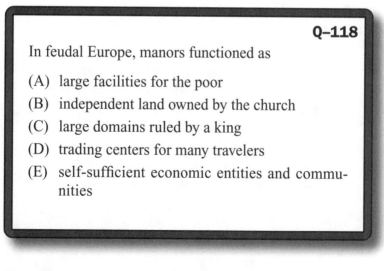

Q–118

In feudal Europe, manors functioned as

(A) large facilities for the poor

(B) independent land owned by the church

(C) large domains ruled by a king

(D) trading centers for many travelers

(E) self-sufficient economic entities and communities

Your Answer _____

Correct Answers

A–117

(D) The growth of corn and maize was the basic foundation of the Mayan economy. These products were traded and provided the staple foods of the Mayan diet. The Mayans used gold as ornamentation in temples but not as a currency.

A–118

(E) Manors were self-contained feudal communities that lords would preside over. Serfs provided labor and skills to produce agricultural goods and also crafts that were needed. For example, a blacksmith or a leatherworker would provide their goods, and these goods could be bartered for foodstuffs. Farmers worked the land and rotated crops under the supervision of the lord and his administration.

Q–119

The Holy Roman Empire evolved as a counterbalance to

(A) Muslim influence in the Balkans

(B) church power in medieval Europe

(C) Viking invasions from the north

(D) Mongol invasions from the East

(E) the power of the Carolingian empire

Your Answer _____

_____

Q–120

During the feudal era in Europe, centralized monarchies began to develop in

(A) the Balkans

(B) Scandinavia

(C) the Holy Roman Empire

(D) the West

(E) the alpine regions

Your Answer _____

_____

Correct Answers

A–119

(B) Pope John XII rewarded a loyal king with the title of Holy Roman Emperor in 962. The empire, which makes up part of present-day Germany, was a patchwork of Christian domains in northern Europe. The title of emperor was sometimes misleading because numerous princes contended with the church and its sanctioned ruler. Numerous power struggles between Rome and the ruler of northern Europe took place as both tried to establish authority.

A–120

(D) Strong centralized monarchies began to appear first in France and Spain after 1050. Powerful families like the Plantagenets in France and England ruled over larger and larger domains. Through war and marriage, these domains were won and lost over time. Larger-scale conflicts, such as the Hundred Years' War, forced monarchies to raise armies and pay for them through more sophisticated taxation policies. By 1400, Spain, France, and England were more developed as nation-states than the rest of the European nations.

Q–121

The monarchy of which European medieval kingdom was represented by the symbol pictured above?

(A) Wales

(B) The Papal States

(C) Scotland

(D) France

(E) Spain

Your Answer _____

_____

Correct Answers

A–121

(D) Although also used by the Muslim ruler of Syria, historically the fleur-de-lis became associated with the monarchy of the kingdom of France. The House of Bourbon, which ruled France for many years, adopted the symbol. As early as 1179, Louis VII used the design during ceremonies. Over time, its use on banners and uniforms became associated with the French king and the Bourbon dynasty.

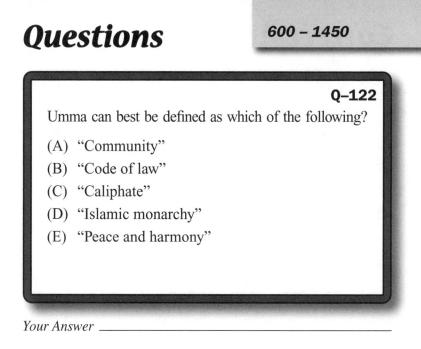

Q–122

Umma can best be defined as which of the following?

(A) "Community"

(B) "Code of law"

(C) "Caliphate"

(D) "Islamic monarchy"

(E) "Peace and harmony"

Your Answer _____

_____

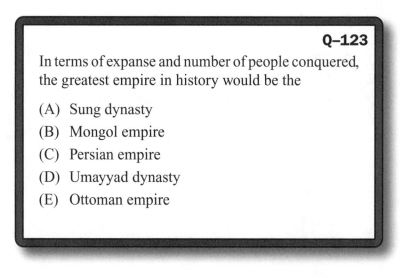

Q–123

In terms of expanse and number of people conquered, the greatest empire in history would be the

(A) Sung dynasty

(B) Mongol empire

(C) Persian empire

(D) Umayyad dynasty

(E) Ottoman empire

Your Answer _____

_____

Correct Answers

A–122

(A) Translated from Arabic as "community or nation," Mohammed and his successors emphasized the extended connectedness of Islam. As it spread, Islam was thought of as a large association of believers brought together by the faith. Referred to in the Koran, umma can be thought of as a unified religious entity joined in belief in Allah and his Prophet.

A–123

(B) The Mongol empire extended from southern China all the way to eastern Europe at its greatest extent c. 1280. After Genghis Khan swept into the Caucasus, his successors continued to conquer South Asia and Russia. Although the Mongol empire did not remain intact for long, it is the most impressive feat of military conquest in human history.

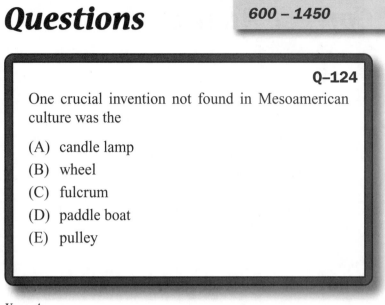

Q–124

One crucial invention not found in Mesoamerican culture was the

(A) candle lamp
(B) wheel
(C) fulcrum
(D) paddle boat
(E) pulley

Your Answer —————————————————————————

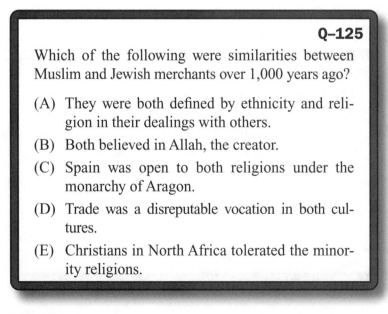

Q–125

Which of the following were similarities between Muslim and Jewish merchants over 1,000 years ago?

(A) They were both defined by ethnicity and religion in their dealings with others.
(B) Both believed in Allah, the creator.
(C) Spain was open to both religions under the monarchy of Aragon.
(D) Trade was a disreputable vocation in both cultures.
(E) Christians in North Africa tolerated the minority religions.

Your Answer —————————————————————————

Correct Answers

A–124

(B) Without the wheel, Mesoamerican tribes and cultures had to rely on pack animals or simple skid sleds pulled by horses. This limited the amount that could be carried and also the speed at which goods could be transported. Even so, the Mayans had roads hundreds of kilometers long that were used to transport goods for trade.

A–125

(A) During the Middle Ages, religious and ethnic identity defined many Muslims and Jews as they traveled and traded throughout Africa and Asia. Both faiths were scattered across three continents 1,000 years ago, and many Muslims and Jews were traders who bought and sold their goods over great distances.

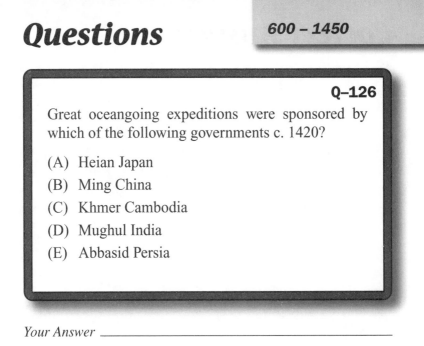

Q–126

Great oceangoing expeditions were sponsored by which of the following governments c. 1420?

(A) Heian Japan

(B) Ming China

(C) Khmer Cambodia

(D) Mughul India

(E) Abbasid Persia

Your Answer _____

_____

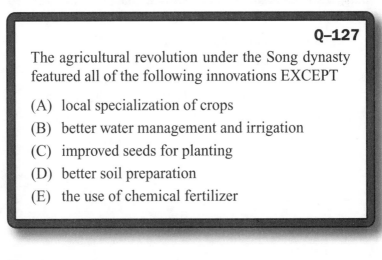

Q–127

The agricultural revolution under the Song dynasty featured all of the following innovations EXCEPT

(A) local specialization of crops

(B) better water management and irrigation

(C) improved seeds for planting

(D) better soil preparation

(E) the use of chemical fertilizer

Your Answer _____

_____

Correct Answers

A–126

(B) Under the command of an admiral named Zheng He, the Ming dynasty built a fleet of impressive ships that traveled throughout Asia and the Indian Ocean. The Chinese exported silk and porcelain to peoples thousands of kilometers from China in the early 1400s.

A–127

(E) Song China saw the improvement of many aspects of farming around 1100. Crops and land were better managed and yields increased. The Chinese used organic fertilizer but did not have access to chemical fertilizer.

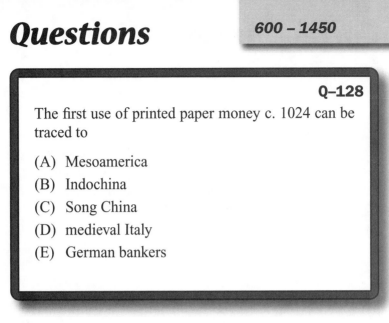

Q–128

The first use of printed paper money c. 1024 can be traced to

(A) Mesoamerica

(B) Indochina

(C) Song China

(D) medieval Italy

(E) German bankers

Your Answer _____

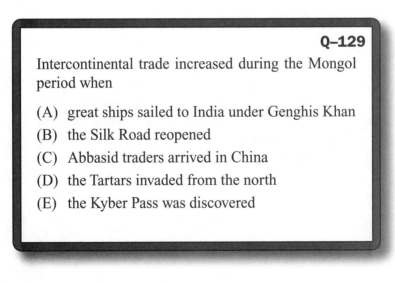

Q–129

Intercontinental trade increased during the Mongol period when

(A) great ships sailed to India under Genghis Khan

(B) the Silk Road reopened

(C) Abbasid traders arrived in China

(D) the Tartars invaded from the north

(E) the Kyber Pass was discovered

Your Answer _____

Correct Answers

A–128

(C) The first money is believed to have been printed in Szechuan China during the Song period. New ways to offer credit to merchants were developed to facilitate trade. Greater market freedom allowed for more goods to change hands, which stimulated business.

A–129

(B) The period sometimes termed Pax Mongolica lasted for about a century and saw the reestablishment of trade routes, including the Silk Road, that spanned Asia. Traders could travel all the way from China to Europe and North Africa at this time.

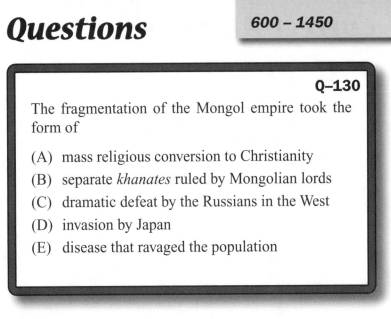

Q–130

The fragmentation of the Mongol empire took the form of

(A) mass religious conversion to Christianity

(B) separate *khanates* ruled by Mongolian lords

(C) dramatic defeat by the Russians in the West

(D) invasion by Japan

(E) disease that ravaged the population

Your Answer _____

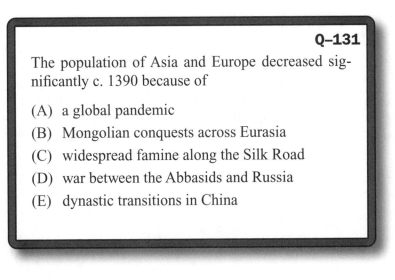

Q–131

The population of Asia and Europe decreased significantly c. 1390 because of

(A) a global pandemic

(B) Mongolian conquests across Eurasia

(C) widespread famine along the Silk Road

(D) war between the Abbasids and Russia

(E) dynastic transitions in China

Your Answer _____

Correct Answers

A–130

(B) With the death of Genghis, the Mongol conquests devolved to separate Mongol relatives who created four separate *khanates.* These *khanates* lasted another generation, until the Mings overthrew the Mongols c. 1368.

A–131

(A) The plague of medieval times is thought to have come with the Mongols to China. It then traveled along trade routes to Europe and decimated the populations there, from south to north. While warfare can account for some deaths in China, millions of deaths are attributed to the plague, from East Asia to Scandinavia.

Questions

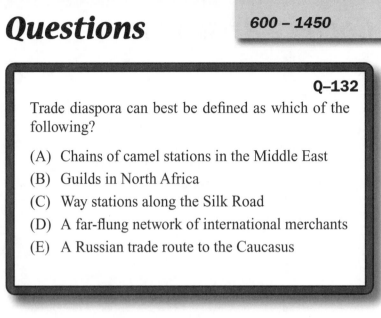

Q-132

Trade diaspora can best be defined as which of the following?

(A) Chains of camel stations in the Middle East

(B) Guilds in North Africa

(C) Way stations along the Silk Road

(D) A far-flung network of international merchants

(E) A Russian trade route to the Caucasus

Your Answer _____

_____

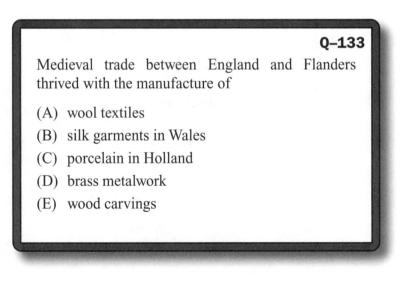

Q-133

Medieval trade between England and Flanders thrived with the manufacture of

(A) wool textiles

(B) silk garments in Wales

(C) porcelain in Holland

(D) brass metalwork

(E) wood carvings

Your Answer _____

_____

Correct Answers

A–132

(D) From ancient times, trade networks extended from the Mediterranean to the Indian Ocean. By 1200, these networks covered three continents. Trade networks also evolved in North America under the Inca by 1450.

A–133

(A) Wool was the most common type of cloth in Europe. The English learned very early to make wool garments and sell them to other parts of Europe. Wool became the foundation of their economy and trade. This in turn earned a favorable balance of trade for England.

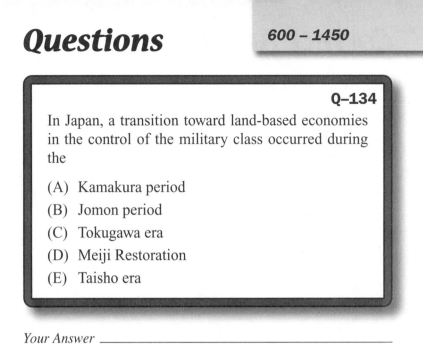

Q–134

In Japan, a transition toward land-based economies in the control of the military class occurred during the

(A) Kamakura period

(B) Jomon period

(C) Tokugawa era

(D) Meiji Restoration

(E) Taisho era

Your Answer _____

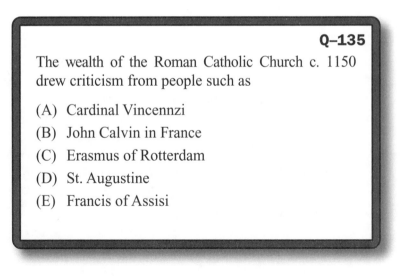

Q–135

The wealth of the Roman Catholic Church c. 1150 drew criticism from people such as

(A) Cardinal Vincennzi

(B) John Calvin in France

(C) Erasmus of Rotterdam

(D) St. Augustine

(E) Francis of Assisi

Your Answer _____

Correct Answers

A–134

(A) After the Heian period, Japan evolved into a feudal order in which an agricultural economy was overseen by the military or samurai class. A *bakufu* government was established in Kamakura around 1185. The head of this government was a shogun who ruled over other feudal lords from west to east.

A–135

(E) Some Christians saw the wealth and ornamentation of the church as a departure from the earlier values of charity and community. Francis of Assisi was drawn to a vision of simple poverty and service for the common people. He sought and received the blessing of the pope to create his own order within the Roman Catholic Church in which priests could take pledges of poverty and work among the poor.

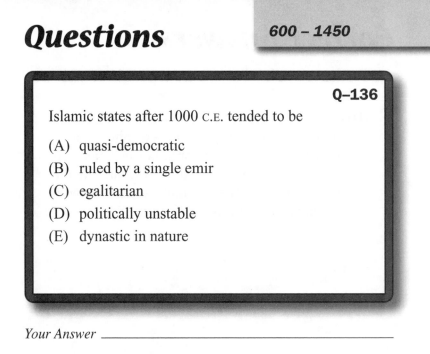

Q–136

Islamic states after 1000 C.E. tended to be

(A) quasi-democratic
(B) ruled by a single emir
(C) egalitarian
(D) politically unstable
(E) dynastic in nature

Your Answer _____

_____

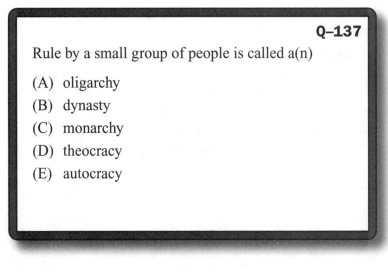

Q–137

Rule by a small group of people is called a(n)

(A) oligarchy
(B) dynasty
(C) monarchy
(D) theocracy
(E) autocracy

Your Answer _____

_____

Correct Answers

A–136

(D) After Islam expanded to its largest membership in 900, it broke into various domains ruled by sultans. Rule was authoritarian and undemocratic. Assassination and internecine conflict was common. The ongoing schism between Sunni and Shia further divided the faith.

A–137

(A) When a nation or kingdom is controlled by a few powerful elites, it is called an oligarchy. This group of elites could be a ruling council or a small class of elites. An oligarchy is an undemocratic situation because the power elites will not give up power to the people.

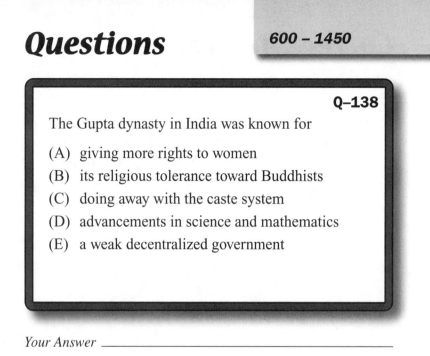

Q–138

The Gupta dynasty in India was known for

(A) giving more rights to women
(B) its religious tolerance toward Buddhists
(C) doing away with the caste system
(D) advancements in science and mathematics
(E) a weak decentralized government

Your Answer _____

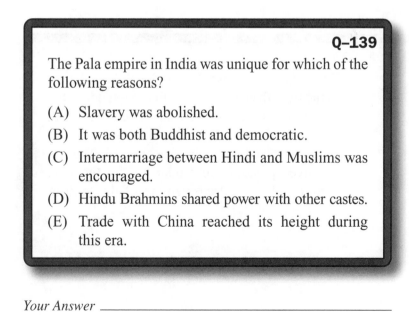

Q–139

The Pala empire in India was unique for which of the following reasons?

(A) Slavery was abolished.
(B) It was both Buddhist and democratic.
(C) Intermarriage between Hindi and Muslims was encouraged.
(D) Hindu Brahmins shared power with other castes.
(E) Trade with China reached its height during this era.

Your Answer _____

Correct Answers

A–138

(D) The Gupta emperor Chandragupta supported scientific study of the heavens and succeeded in calculating the timing and frequency of solar eclipses. It was a thoroughly Hindu regime that retained the caste system.

A–139

(B) The Pala empire lasted from the eighth century to the twelfth century in South Asia. It consisted of the present-day Bihar and Bengal regions in the north. Gopala, the first emperor, was an independent Buddhist who was elected. The aggressive spreading of Buddhism by the Pala empire led to the transplanting of the faith to Tibet in the north.

Questions

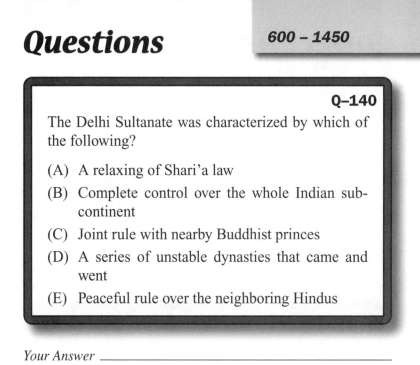

Q–140

The Delhi Sultanate was characterized by which of the following?

(A) A relaxing of Shari'a law

(B) Complete control over the whole Indian sub-continent

(C) Joint rule with nearby Buddhist princes

(D) A series of unstable dynasties that came and went

(E) Peaceful rule over the neighboring Hindus

Your Answer _____

_____

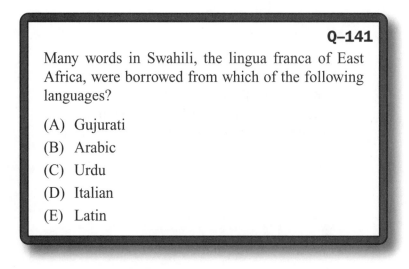

Q–141

Many words in Swahili, the lingua franca of East Africa, were borrowed from which of the following languages?

(A) Gujurati

(B) Arabic

(C) Urdu

(D) Italian

(E) Latin

Your Answer _____

_____

Correct Answers

A–140

(D) Violence and instability were a hallmark of the Delhi Sultanate, which ruled portions of northern India roughly from 1200 to 1500. Many of the sultans were assassinated along the way, and rebellious Hindu princes did not accept the foreign power and its foreign religion.

A–141

(B) Arab traders had important influences on African culture, and it is believed that up to 20 percent of Swahili words are derived from Arabic. Extensive contact between Muslim traders on the coast of East Africa made considerable cultural transfer possible.

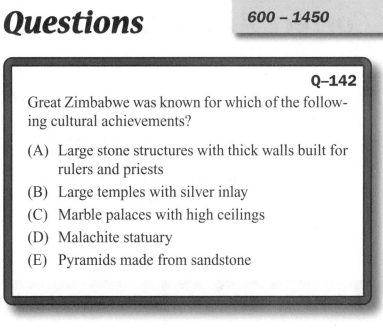

Q–142

Great Zimbabwe was known for which of the following cultural achievements?

(A) Large stone structures with thick walls built for rulers and priests
(B) Large temples with silver inlay
(C) Marble palaces with high ceilings
(D) Malachite statuary
(E) Pyramids made from sandstone

Your Answer _____

_____

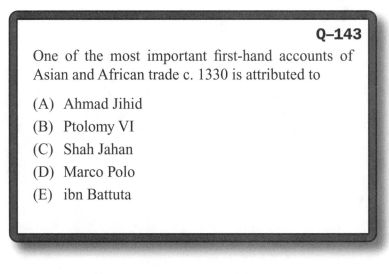

Q–143

One of the most important first-hand accounts of Asian and African trade c. 1330 is attributed to

(A) Ahmad Jihid
(B) Ptolomy VI
(C) Shah Jahan
(D) Marco Polo
(E) ibn Battuta

Your Answer _____

_____

Correct Answers

A–142

(A) A center of trade in southern Africa was a city called Great Zimbabwe. Here archeologists have uncovered large stone areas, some the size of modern sports stadiums. Walls up to 15 feet thick were built for the ruling elite of the city. These ruins are some of the most impressive in sub-Saharan Africa.

A–143

(E) The accounts of the Muslim ibn Battuta are some of the best historical descriptions of Africa and Asia in the medieval period. Originally traveling to Mecca on a pilgrimage, ibn Battuta continued his travels until he had visited most of North Africa, parts of Europe, and many areas of Asia.

Questions

Q–144

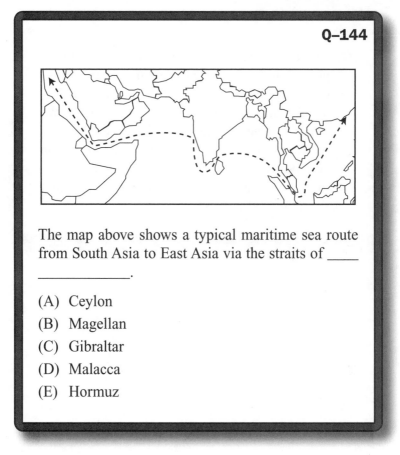

The map above shows a typical maritime sea route from South Asia to East Asia via the straits of _____
_____.

(A) Ceylon

(B) Magellan

(C) Gibraltar

(D) Malacca

(E) Hormuz

Your Answer _____

Correct Answers

A–144

(D) The most logical route through the East Indies goes from the Indian Ocean through the Straits of Malacca. This narrow route between the Malayan peninsula and the island of Java allowed seagoing trade to pass from India to China for many centuries. This made Malacca an important port, especially after the ruler converted to Islam, which in turn encouraged more trade from the Middle East.

Questions

Q–145

Which of the following is associated with the spread of Islam in sub-Saharan Africa?

(A) Mass conversions of Hindu traders

(B) The carving of mosques out of solid rock in Ethiopia

(C) The borrowing of many Swahili words from Arabic

(D) The spread of literacy because reading the Quran was encouraged

(E) Increased tension between African princes and Muslim traders

Your Answer _____

Q–146

One reason for the spread of Islam can be traced to the common practice of

(A) polygamy

(B) infanticide

(C) bigamy

(D) monogamy

(E) slavery

Your Answer _____

Correct Answers

A–145

(D) Muslim converts in Africa were encouraged to learn Arabic so they could read the scriptures in the original. The memorization of the Quran is a traditional activity within Islam, and being able to read Arabic facilitated this activity. This caused literacy to rise in central Africa because many Africans converted to Islam. Eventually Quranic schools were founded to encourage the study of Muslim theology and culture.

A–146

(A) The practice of polygamy among Muslims meant that one man could father a large number of children and all of them would be raised in the Islamic faith. Concubines and slaves might also be converted to Islam. This was one factor that increased both the birthrate and the number of Muslims over time.

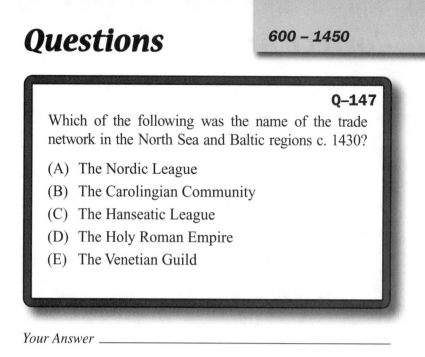

Q–147

Which of the following was the name of the trade network in the North Sea and Baltic regions c. 1430?

(A) The Nordic League

(B) The Carolingian Community

(C) The Hanseatic League

(D) The Holy Roman Empire

(E) The Venetian Guild

Your Answer _____

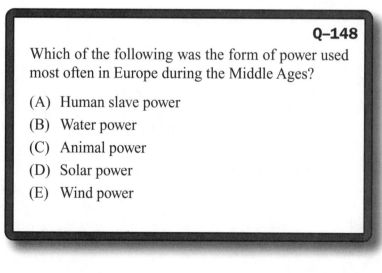

Q–148

Which of the following was the form of power used most often in Europe during the Middle Ages?

(A) Human slave power

(B) Water power

(C) Animal power

(D) Solar power

(E) Wind power

Your Answer _____

Correct Answers

A–147

(C) The Hanseatic League was a trade association, with trading cities across northern Europe, at the end of the Middle Ages. Cities such as Hamburg and Bremen entered into commercial agreements that allowed more modern banking systems to develop. The merchant classes in the German states, Holland, and Poland grew, which in turn allowed for more upward mobility.

A–148

(B) The use of water mills became very common during the Middle Ages in many parts of Europe. The channeling of water became more sophisticated, as did the wheels that were turned by the water. Wheat could be ground and metal could be stamped using water power for the production of food and other products.

Q–149

The term *chivalry* can best be defined as which of the following?

(A) A code of behavior and ethics for nobles during the medieval era

(B) A system of taxation devised in Italy

(C) Exemption of slaves from certain kinds of work

(D) Extending citizenship to conquered peoples

(E) Fighting neighboring domains for more territory

Your Answer _____

Q–150

What minority group in Europe and Asia sometimes suffered persecution because of their status as outsiders in Christian and Muslim society?

(A) The Rus

(B) The Armenians

(C) The Shiites

(D) The Swiss

(E) The Jews

Your Answer _____

Correct Answers

A–149

(A) Chivalry was a code of honor for nobles who fought during the Middle Ages. At first these groups were more focused on warrior communities, but later they came to resemble some of the monastic orders of the church. The mythic Round Table of King Arthur is an expression of this devotion to honor and duty as a knight. Chivalry also exalted women and made men their protectors.

A–150

(E) Belonging to neither the mainstream Latin Christian church in the West nor the Muslim faith in the East, Jews were outsiders in many respects during the Middle Ages. Sometimes Jews were forced to convert to another faith under duress, but many would continue to practice their faith in secret. Given the Christian and Muslim prohibition of lending money and charging interest, some Jews went into the banking and finance sector. Periodic discrimination and suspicion of the Jews became a feature of their lives in Europe and elsewhere.

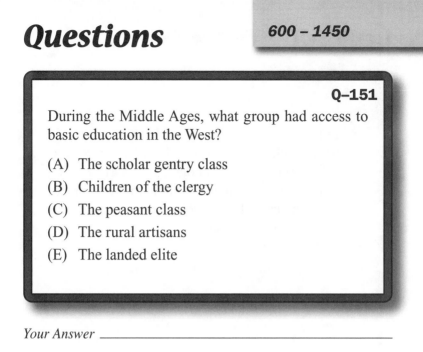

Q–151

During the Middle Ages, what group had access to basic education in the West?

(A) The scholar gentry class

(B) Children of the clergy

(C) The peasant class

(D) The rural artisans

(E) The landed elite

Your Answer _____

_____

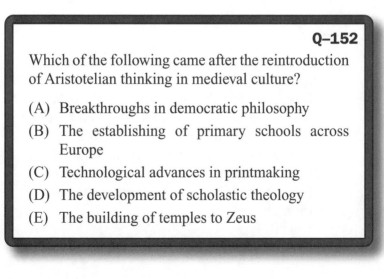

Q–152

Which of the following came after the reintroduction of Aristotelian thinking in medieval culture?

(A) Breakthroughs in democratic philosophy

(B) The establishing of primary schools across Europe

(C) Technological advances in printmaking

(D) The development of scholastic theology

(E) The building of temples to Zeus

Your Answer _____

_____

Correct Answers

A–151

(E) Basic education was rare in the medieval era in Europe. Some children of landed families would have monks tutor their children. Even rarer was the establishment of scholars in a court by a king or lord who was interested in learning. Some of the cathedral schools evolved into the early universities, but these served only the elite.

A–152

(D) During the Middle Ages, church thinkers and philosophers began to incorporate classical ideas into their theology. At first Plato had a greater impact, but later Aristotle, with his emphasis on logic and reason, began to influence Christian theology. Scholasticism is the school of theology that developed from this synthesis of ancient pre-Christian thinking and the medieval faith.

Q–153

Which of the following was the trade that the kingdom of Ghana was built upon around the eleventh century?

(A) Salt

(B) Gold

(C) Glassware

(D) Silver

(E) Cyprus wood

Your Answer _____

_____

Q–154

Which of the following African empires controlled the trade of West Africa beginning in the thirteenth century?

(A) The kingdom of Ghana

(B) The Mali empire

(C) The Abbasid empire

(D) The Persian empire

(E) The Zambezi empire

Your Answer _____

_____

Correct Answers

A–153

(B) Although the old kingdom of Ghana (no relation to the present-day nation), did not produce gold, it became a trading center where the precious metal was bought and sold. Coming from regions to the south near the Senegal and Gambia rivers, gold was traded in nugget form by many merchants from throughout North Africa. The kings of Ghana controlled the trade and taxing of the gold, and they became rich and powerful over time.

A–154

(B) The Mali empire dominated trade between North and West Africa for almost three centuries, beginning around 1270. The lion prince Sundiata had built up his domain by making alliances with other rulers and creating a large military force. The taxes from the trade that took place enriched the treasury of the Mali empire.

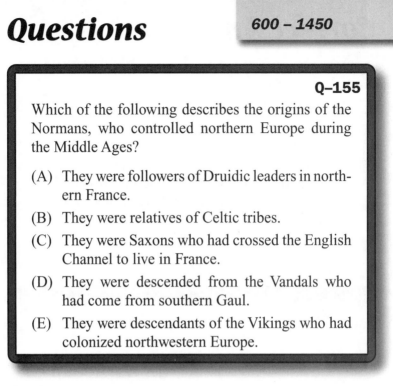

Q–155

Which of the following describes the origins of the Normans, who controlled northern Europe during the Middle Ages?

(A) They were followers of Druidic leaders in northern France.

(B) They were relatives of Celtic tribes.

(C) They were Saxons who had crossed the English Channel to live in France.

(D) They were descended from the Vandals who had come from southern Gaul.

(E) They were descendants of the Vikings who had colonized northwestern Europe.

Your Answer _____

_____

Q–156

Chinampa can best be described as which of the following?

(A) Migrant workers who served the king

(B) Royal elites who ruled the Toltecs

(C) Trading caravans that existed in Mesoamerica

(D) Plots of land enriched with lake bottom soil

(E) Boats for fishing on lakes

Your Answer _____

_____

Correct Answers

A–155

(E) *Norman* is a variation of *northmen*, who were Vikings who stayed in northern France to live and rule. They established themselves after 800 and became part of the feudal order. Converting to Christianity, Norman leaders such as William of Normandy carved out domains in that part of France.

A–156

(D) Agriculture was enhanced in ancient Mexico when a new approach to soil application gave rise to the *chinampa* system of growing crops. Farmers dredged the bottom of the lake for the rich muck and applied it to their fields. This nutrient-rich soil allowed many crops to be grown per year, thus increasing yields.

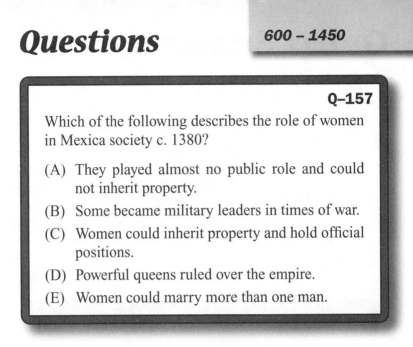

Q–157

Which of the following describes the role of women in Mexica society c. 1380?

(A) They played almost no public role and could not inherit property.

(B) Some became military leaders in times of war.

(C) Women could inherit property and hold official positions.

(D) Powerful queens ruled over the empire.

(E) Women could marry more than one man.

Your Answer _____

_____

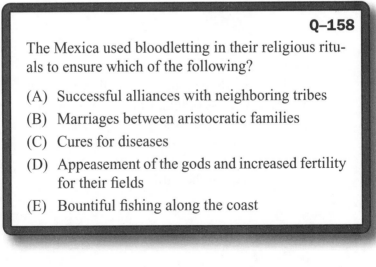

Q–158

The Mexica used bloodletting in their religious rituals to ensure which of the following?

(A) Successful alliances with neighboring tribes

(B) Marriages between aristocratic families

(C) Cures for diseases

(D) Appeasement of the gods and increased fertility for their fields

(E) Bountiful fishing along the coast

Your Answer _____

_____

Correct Answers

A–157

(A) Women in Mexica over a thousand years ago could not serve in the military nor could they inherit property. Although they played a commercial role in marketplaces, they were encouraged more toward motherhood and caring for the home. This patriarchal culture limited women severely in terms of their roles in society.

A–158

(D) The people known as the Mexica absorbed religious practices from the Mesoamerican culture around them. They associated the flow of blood with the moistness of the earth. This was needed for the growing of their staple crops: maize and corn. They honored their deities by using human sacrifice and the letting of blood to encourage the fertility of the earth.

Q–159

Which of the following represent the medieval reform movements within the Roman Catholic Church?

(A) Calvinist princes who challenged Rome

(B) The Knights Templar, who fought for the pope

(C) Norman lords who petitioned Rome

(D) Scholastic monks who emphasized knowledge over faith

(E) Mendicant orders like the Franciscans, who took oaths of poverty

Your Answer _____

Q–160

Which of the following is an example of agricultural diffusion in the medieval period?

(A) The growing of coffee in France after the Great Schism

(B) Crusaders bringing sugar back from the Middle East

(C) African traders introducing maize to India

(D) Celtic slaves showing salt to Germans

(E) Moorish invaders bringing bananas to Spain

Your Answer _____

Correct Answers

A-159

(E) As the Roman Catholic Church became more powerful and wealthy, some Christians reacted against the temporal nature of the church. Dominic and Francis of Assisi vowed to leave worldly cares behind and devote themselves to charitable work with the poorest people. This was a reformist reaction against the corruption they saw in the church. They saw their lives of simplicity as being more Christ-like because they depended completely on God for their needs.

A-160

(B) The movements of armies have often been instrumental in bringing foodstuffs to other parts of the world. The Crusades brought thousands of soldiers from western Europe to western Asia, where they tasted foods and additives that were unknown at home. Sugar was an Arab sweetener that was outside the experience of the Europeans, who had only honey to make their foods sweet. This led to the growing of sugar cane in the Mediterranean to ensure that Europe had a supply of the sweetener.

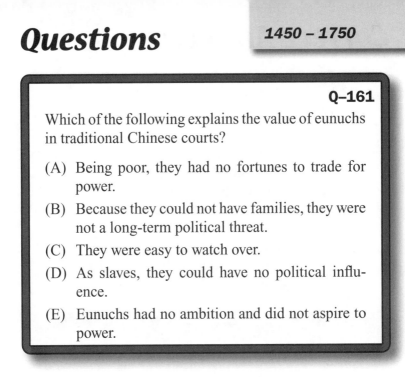

Q–161

Which of the following explains the value of eunuchs in traditional Chinese courts?

(A) Being poor, they had no fortunes to trade for power.

(B) Because they could not have families, they were not a long-term political threat.

(C) They were easy to watch over.

(D) As slaves, they could have no political influence.

(E) Eunuchs had no ambition and did not aspire to power.

Your Answer _____

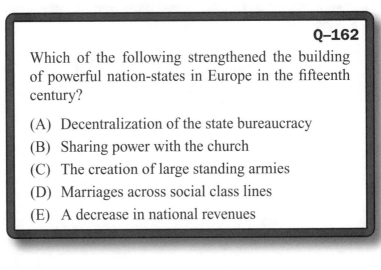

Q–162

Which of the following strengthened the building of powerful nation-states in Europe in the fifteenth century?

(A) Decentralization of the state bureaucracy

(B) Sharing power with the church

(C) The creation of large standing armies

(D) Marriages across social class lines

(E) A decrease in national revenues

Your Answer _____

Correct Answers

A–161

(B) The Ming dynasty employed eunuchs in the court to a greater extent than did previous dynasties. Because eunuchs were neutered, they could not have children and thus could not establish any familial legacy. Chinese families were based on the patriarchal power base that went from father to son. Eunuchs did gain great amounts of power and influence, however, in certain courts in China. They could be skillful bureaucrats and sometimes even well-known warriors.

A–162

(C) Regional monarchies in western Europe were able to consolidate and increase their power through both taxation and the maintaining of large military. By 1500, armies of over 10,000 professional soldiers were created and supplied with firearms by powerful kings.

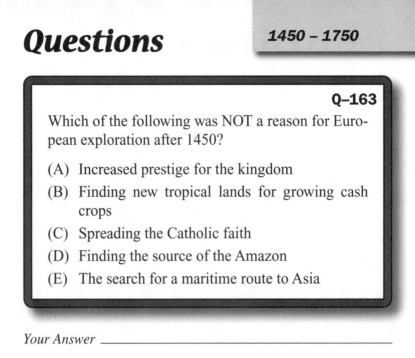

Q–163

Which of the following was NOT a reason for European exploration after 1450?

(A) Increased prestige for the kingdom

(B) Finding new tropical lands for growing cash crops

(C) Spreading the Catholic faith

(D) Finding the source of the Amazon

(E) The search for a maritime route to Asia

Your Answer _____

_____

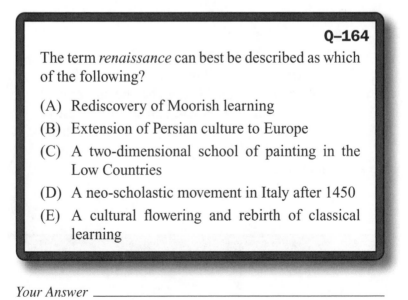

Q–164

The term *renaissance* can best be described as which of the following?

(A) Rediscovery of Moorish learning

(B) Extension of Persian culture to Europe

(C) A two-dimensional school of painting in the Low Countries

(D) A neo-scholastic movement in Italy after 1450

(E) A cultural flowering and rebirth of classical learning

Your Answer _____

_____

Correct Answers

A–163

(D) With the increased demand for products from Asia, explorers sought a sea route to India and China. Prices for silk and spices were so high that a voyage could pay for itself many times over. Eventually, foreign claims would boost national prestige and serve as areas where European cultures could be transplanted in the Americas, Africa, and Asia.

A–164

(E) The term *renaissance* actually is translated as "rebirth" and is used to describe an era of early modern European history that begins around 1450. Starting in Italy, it spread to the rest of western Europe and framed new ways of artistic expression that encompassed art, music, and architecture.

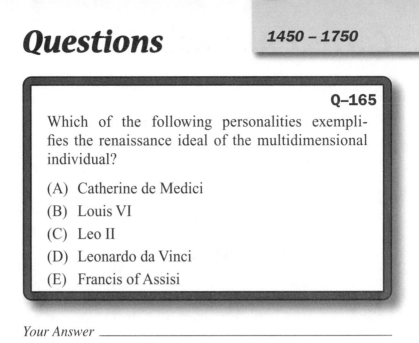

Q–165

Which of the following personalities exemplifies the renaissance ideal of the multidimensional individual?

(A) Catherine de Medici

(B) Louis VI

(C) Leo II

(D) Leonardo da Vinci

(E) Francis of Assisi

Your Answer _____

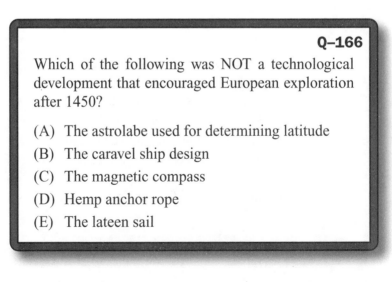

Q–166

Which of the following was NOT a technological development that encouraged European exploration after 1450?

(A) The astrolabe used for determining latitude

(B) The caravel ship design

(C) The magnetic compass

(D) Hemp anchor rope

(E) The lateen sail

Your Answer _____

Correct Answers

A–165

(D) Leonardo da Vinci came to represent the new man celebrated in the Italian Renaissance. His lifetime of study and observation made him an artist, musician, engineer, and scientist. Patronized by powerful Italian princes, Leonardo painted, sculpted, and invented. His notebooks show drawings that anticipated technologies that would not appear for centuries.

A–166

(D) Various advances in ship design and navigation made it easier to sail longer distances on the high seas after 1400. Hemp had been used for some time in making rope, but the new sail shapes meant ships could maneuver in different winds. The new science and technology meant that the ocean was less mysterious, and explorers ventured farther and farther from their home ports.

Q-167

Humanists were affected by which of the following ideas at the start of the Renaissance?

(A) Scholastic theology

(B) Greek and Roman values and approaches

(C) Gallic literature

(D) Medieval customs

(E) Hebraic legal systems

Your Answer _____

Q-168

Which of the following explains the new prosperity of Italian domains and cities after 1400?

(A) Trade flourished and enriched the merchant classes.

(B) The pope had a monopoly on certain goods.

(C) Spanish merchants sold Asian goods to the rest of Europe.

(D) Moorish princes overpaid for Italian goods.

(E) The Holy Roman Empire was a trading cross-roads.

Your Answer _____

Correct Answers

A–167

(B) Humanists such as Erasmus of Rotterdam sought a departure from the medieval worldview and rediscovered many works of the ancient classical thinkers. Philosophy from Athens and Rome enhanced the traditional beliefs. Works that had been unstudied for centuries were uncovered and shared by scholars.

A–168

(A) Italian ports and cities were ideally located to become trading centers as goods flowed from Asia to the rest of Europe. Traders went farther and farther in search of goods that Europeans wanted. Profits rose as the population of Europe grew, thus creating more demand.

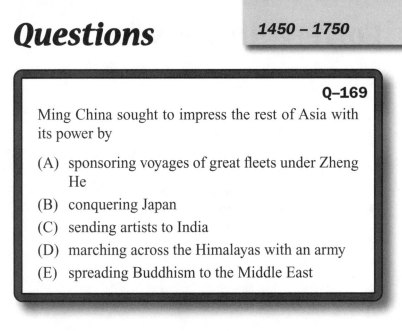

Q–169

Ming China sought to impress the rest of Asia with its power by

(A) sponsoring voyages of great fleets under Zheng He

(B) conquering Japan

(C) sending artists to India

(D) marching across the Himalayas with an army

(E) spreading Buddhism to the Middle East

Your Answer _____

_____

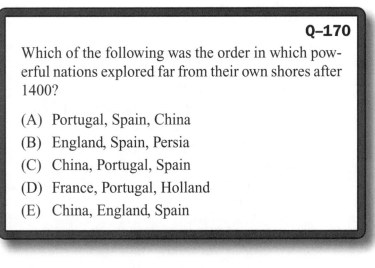

Q–170

Which of the following was the order in which powerful nations explored far from their own shores after 1400?

(A) Portugal, Spain, China

(B) England, Spain, Persia

(C) China, Portugal, Spain

(D) France, Portugal, Holland

(E) China, England, Spain

Your Answer _____

_____

Correct Answers

A-169

(A) At the height of Ming power, the emperor Yongle sent out his admiral Zheng He to sail the South China Sea and Indian Ocean. The largest ships ever built could hold hundreds of passengers, and the Chinese traded with India, Africa, and Ceylon. Gifts were exchanged with other rulers, and China showed that its maritime powers rivaled anyone else's in that century.

A-170

(C) Ming China sent out large fleets to explore the Indian Ocean and was followed by the Portuguese, who sailed to India via the Cape. In competition with Portugal, the kingdom of Spain sent its fleets west to seek another route to Asia. Ming China gave up oceanic exploration and trade shortly after, but the Europeans began to sail to the New World and competed for colonies and riches.

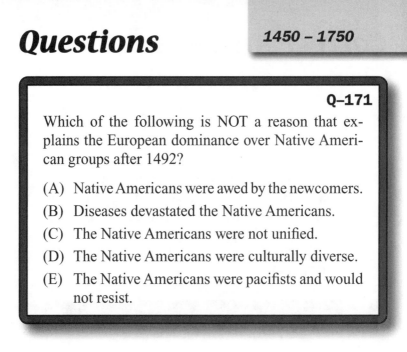

Q–171

Which of the following is NOT a reason that explains the European dominance over Native American groups after 1492?

(A) Native Americans were awed by the newcomers.

(B) Diseases devastated the Native Americans.

(C) The Native Americans were not unified.

(D) The Native Americans were culturally diverse.

(E) The Native Americans were pacifists and would not resist.

Your Answer _____

_____

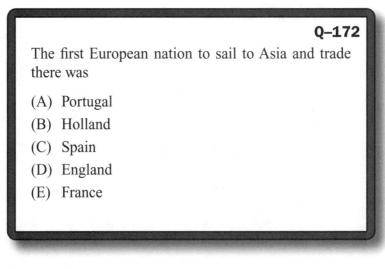

Q–172

The first European nation to sail to Asia and trade there was

(A) Portugal

(B) Holland

(C) Spain

(D) England

(E) France

Your Answer _____

_____

Correct Answers

A–171

(E) Most Native American groups were experienced in fighting when the Spanish arrived in 1492. But fighting was difficult when the whites could play one Native American group off another. They had sophisticated forms of government and some tribes were confederated, but the diseases brought by Europeans decreased native populations by more than half within a century of Columbus's landing.

A–172

(A) Desiring to profit from maritime exploration, Prince Henry of Portugal was the first to send ships out to explore. The Portuguese colonized the Azores and other island groups in the North Atlantic and then headed down the coast of Africa. Eventually, they rounded the Cape and were in the Indian Ocean. This gave them access to south Asia and the profitable trade goods found there.

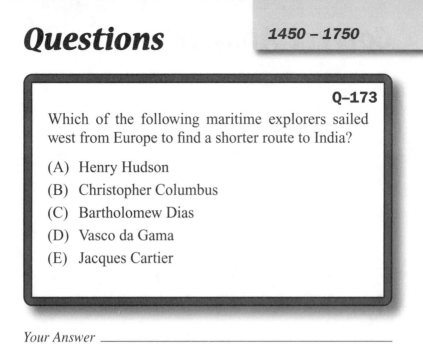

Q–173

Which of the following maritime explorers sailed west from Europe to find a shorter route to India?

(A) Henry Hudson

(B) Christopher Columbus

(C) Bartholomew Dias

(D) Vasco da Gama

(E) Jacques Cartier

Your Answer _____

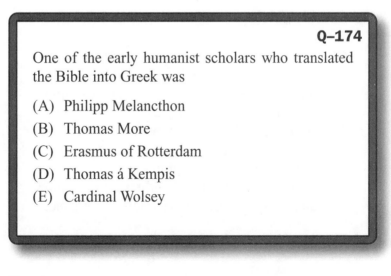

Q–174

One of the early humanist scholars who translated the Bible into Greek was

(A) Philipp Melancthon

(B) Thomas More

(C) Erasmus of Rotterdam

(D) Thomas á Kempis

(E) Cardinal Wolsey

Your Answer _____

Correct Answers

A–173

(B) Columbus was Italian and researched the maps and logs of other navigators to hypothesize that the world was actually small and round. He believed if he sailed due west from Europe he could reach Asia in a month or so. He was mistaken, but he did reach the Caribbean in six weeks.

A–174

(C) Erasmus of Rotterdam set a standard for humanistic scholarship in the 1400s. He read Latin and Greek, which allowed him to explore the ancient texts from antiquity. He applied the learning of Athens and Rome to his understanding of Christianity and raised questions about the accuracy of the Scriptures as they were then translated. He mentored and encouraged other humanists, such as Thomas More of England.

Q–175

Which of the following aided the Europeans as they sailed farther and farther from home in the Age of Discovery?

(A) Calm seas along their sea routes

(B) Knowledge of winds and currents

(C) Navigational help from Pacific islanders

(D) Well-armed ships of war

(E) Jesuit priests who served as ambassadors

Your Answer _____

Q–176

The term *conquistador* is translated as

(A) explorer

(B) conqueror

(C) navigator

(D) inquisitor

(E) missionary

Your Answer _____

Correct Answers

A–175

(B) Once the Atlantic and Pacific were part of the experience of European sailors, they made their own observations about the winds and movement of the seas. They charted the trade winds and noted the latitudes. This allowed them to find routes where winds were favorable depending on the directions they were going in.

A–176

(B) After explorers like Columbus claimed the New World for Spain, other kinds of military expeditions were sent out to learn more about the new territories. Cortes, Pizarro, and de Soto went to different parts of the Americas seeking riches and knowledge about a continent completely unknown to Europe. These aggressive soldiers explored and also laid the groundwork for the conquest of the natives they encountered.

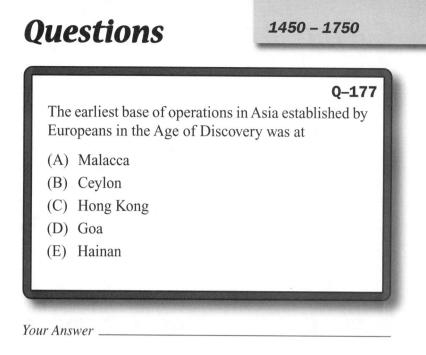

Q–177

The earliest base of operations in Asia established by Europeans in the Age of Discovery was at

(A) Malacca

(B) Ceylon

(C) Hong Kong

(D) Goa

(E) Hainan

Your Answer _____

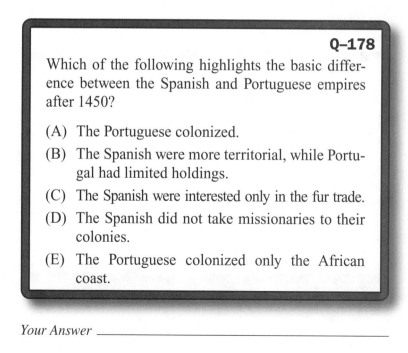

Q–178

Which of the following highlights the basic difference between the Spanish and Portuguese empires after 1450?

(A) The Portuguese colonized.

(B) The Spanish were more territorial, while Portugal had limited holdings.

(C) The Spanish were interested only in the fur trade.

(D) The Spanish did not take missionaries to their colonies.

(E) The Portuguese colonized only the African coast.

Your Answer _____

Correct Answers

A–177

(D) The Portuguese were the first to sail to India after the voyage of Vasco da Gama. Later, they established a small base and colony on the west coast of India at Goa. There, spices and other Asian goods were bought and taken back to Europe for sale. This colony remained in Portuguese hands for centuries.

A–178

(B) While the Portuguese ventured to Asia before the Spanish, the discovery of the New World gave Spain a much larger amount of claimed land after 1492. The Portuguese had a modest amount of land over time in Brazil and Africa, while Spain established colonies in Asia and Africa, as well as in North and South America.

Q–179

Which of the following explains the prevalence of European witch-hunts in the early modern era?

(A) Europeans were influenced both by Christianity and folk superstition.

(B) Women were seen as morally superior to men.

(C) Social harmony led to women being accused of spirit worship.

(D) Druid priests controlled popular beliefs about the spirit world.

(E) Protestant doctrine had set ideas about female authority.

Your Answer _____

Q–180

The first kingdom to sponsor the successful circumnavigation of the globe was

(A) Portugal

(B) England

(C) Ming China

(D) Holland

(E) Spain

Your Answer _____

Correct Answers

A–179

(A) Both Christianity and folk superstition fostered belief in the spirit world and the evil forces that preyed on the weak. Women were seen as morally susceptible to these forces, and in a patriarchal culture, they were vulnerable to accusations of witchcraft. The biblical image of woman as temptress and beguiler of man also played into the idea of them having dangerous powers. Tens of thousands of trials took place, and many women were burned at the stake.

A–180

(E) In 1519, Magellan was sponsored by Spain, and he sailed west with five ships. This resulted in the first circling of the globe by an exploring nation. Only one of the five ships made it around the world, and Magellan did not survive the trip. It established the Spanish as a Pacific power, however, and increased their claims around the world.

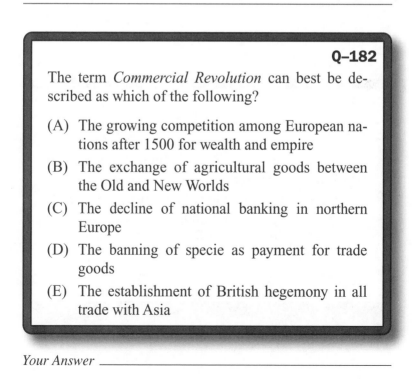

Q–181

Which of the following pairs of nations followed Portugal in establishing trading posts in Asia?

(A) Austria and France

(B) England and Holland

(C) Spain and Germany

(D) Holland and Denmark

(E) Spain and Poland

Your Answer _____

Q–182

The term *Commercial Revolution* can best be described as which of the following?

(A) The growing competition among European nations after 1500 for wealth and empire

(B) The exchange of agricultural goods between the Old and New Worlds

(C) The decline of national banking in northern Europe

(D) The banning of specie as payment for trade goods

(E) The establishment of British hegemony in all trade with Asia

Your Answer _____

Correct Answers

A–181

(B) The Portuguese could not maintain a strong maritime empire partly because Portugal was a small kingdom with limited resources. Holland and England, however, had well-developed financial institutions that were willing to invest in overseas trade. The Dutch and English began to sail to Asia and set up trading posts in the East Indies (later called the Dutch East Indies) and India. This trade led to long-term commitments by both maritime nations that lasted until the mid-twentieth century.

A–182

(A) The modern economic order was framed by the Commercial Revolution after 1500. Large colonial empires gave rise to more sophisticated financial institutions, and corporations were formed to organize large-scale businesses. Joint-stock companies were organized to allow investors to share in the profits of overseas trade.

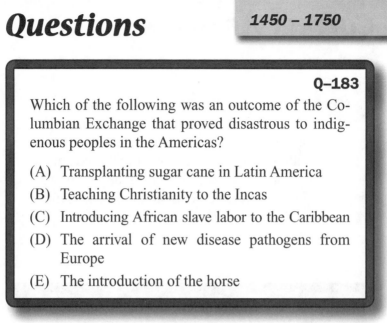

Q–183

Which of the following was an outcome of the Columbian Exchange that proved disastrous to indigenous peoples in the Americas?

(A) Transplanting sugar cane in Latin America

(B) Teaching Christianity to the Incas

(C) Introducing African slave labor to the Caribbean

(D) The arrival of new disease pathogens from Europe

(E) The introduction of the horse

Your Answer _____

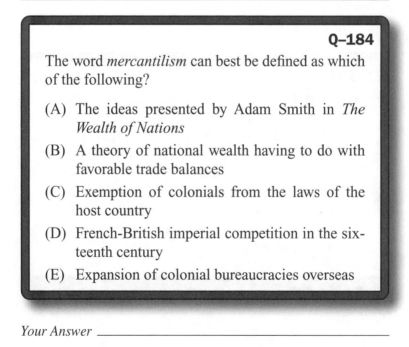

Q–184

The word *mercantilism* can best be defined as which of the following?

(A) The ideas presented by Adam Smith in *The Wealth of Nations*

(B) A theory of national wealth having to do with favorable trade balances

(C) Exemption of colonials from the laws of the host country

(D) French-British imperial competition in the sixteenth century

(E) Expansion of colonial bureaucracies overseas

Your Answer _____

Correct Answers

A–183

(D) Large demographic declines took place across North and South America when European diseases were passed on to natives. Illnesses such as smallpox and influenza killed entire communities in some places, and many of the victims were young children. Some tribal groups and civilizations lost up to 90 percent of their people.

A–184

(B) After 1500, leading European nations adopted an economic theory that national wealth could be gained through a favorable trade balance. This meant that overseas empires could benefit a nation by supplying raw materials for manufacture. These goods could then be sold overseas and money would flow back to the European nation. More exports and fewer imports would be the end result.

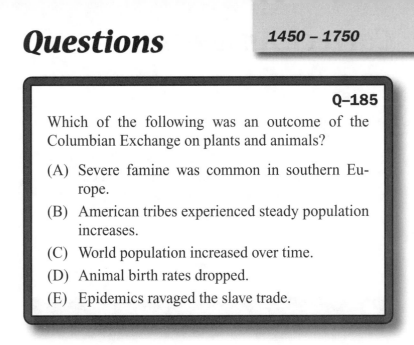

Q–185

Which of the following was an outcome of the Columbian Exchange on plants and animals?

(A) Severe famine was common in southern Europe.

(B) American tribes experienced steady population increases.

(C) World population increased over time.

(D) Animal birth rates dropped.

(E) Epidemics ravaged the slave trade.

Your Answer _____

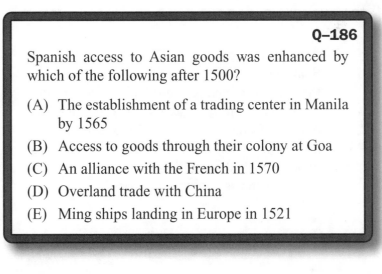

Q–186

Spanish access to Asian goods was enhanced by which of the following after 1500?

(A) The establishment of a trading center in Manila by 1565

(B) Access to goods through their colony at Goa

(C) An alliance with the French in 1570

(D) Overland trade with China

(E) Ming ships landing in Europe in 1521

Your Answer _____

Correct Answers

A–185

(C) The introduction of new crops such as the potato made cheap foodstuffs available to many people. Peasant families could cultivate new sources of carbohydrates that nourished their children. In 1450, Europe was still recovering from the medieval plague, but then it saw a 25 percent increase in population by 1600.

A–186

(A) After Magellan claimed the Philippines for Spain in 1521, other expeditions followed with the purpose of taking control of the archipelago. Missionary priests set about converting the Filipinos to Catholicism. After 1565, a trade connection with Asia and the Americas was formed, with Spanish ships sailing from Manila to Acapulco for transshipment to Europe.

Q–187

The Manila Galleons that sailed from East Asia to the Americas were a component of

(A) revolution during the Renaissance

(B) the slave trade in China

(C) maritime warfare in the Pacific Ocean

(D) global trade in the early modern era

(E) neo-colonialism in the Pacific

Your Answer _____

_____

Q–188

Which of the following practices did NOT cause the fragmentation of the Roman Catholic Church after 1517?

(A) Demonstrations of the wealth of the church

(B) A decline in morality within the priesthood

(C) The sale of indulgences

(D) Challenges to papal authority by regional princes

(E) A growing belief in witches in western Europe

Your Answer _____

_____

Correct Answers

A–187

(D) After the Spanish established a base in East Asia—in the Philippines—they began to cross the Pacific and link with their American holdings in New Spain. They could then span the globe and trade goods with the Chinese. Silver was in great demand in China during the late Ming dynasty, so metals from the New World were brought to Asia for sale.

A–188

(E) By 1500, many felt that the Roman Catholic Church had become corrupt and overly concerned with worldly affairs. Great wealth and power had been accumulated by the Roman Catholic Church and with it came problems such as greed and hypocrisy. Martin Luther was an obscure monk in northern Germany who began a public discussion about the need for the church to reform itself.

Q–189

Which of the following is an example of social hierarchy in the Spanish empire after 1500?

(A) The death of natives who contracted diseases from the conquistadores

(B) The political dominance of the *peninsulares*

(C) The increasing power of the indigenous peoples in Mexico

(D) The abolition of slavery in New Spain after 1550

(E) An emerging middle class made up of mulattos

Your Answer _____

_____

Q–190

Which of the following were Catholic missionary orders that came to the New World to convert the natives to Christianity?

(A) Jesuits and Anglicans

(B) Dominicans and Lutherans

(C) Calvinists and Franciscans

(D) Jesuits and Dominicans

(E) Baptists and Templars

Your Answer _____

_____

Correct Answers

A–189

(B) The social hierarchy of the Spanish in the New World was based on where one was born. Those born in Europe, called the *peninsulares*, were given the highest rank and also the best posts in the New World. The creoles were those born in the Americas, and then there were people of mixed background, slaves, and natives.

A–190

(D) Jesuit and Dominican missionaries accompanied the early Spanish explorers and afterward came to the New World to establish missions. Churches were built and Christianity—in the form of Roman Catholicism—was taught throughout South and North America. Some natives converted, but many also combined their pre-Christian beliefs with the new religion to create a hybrid religion.

Questions

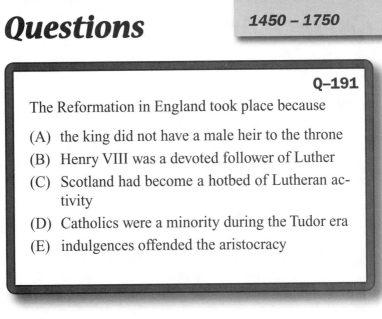

Q–191

The Reformation in England took place because

(A) the king did not have a male heir to the throne
(B) Henry VIII was a devoted follower of Luther
(C) Scotland had become a hotbed of Lutheran activity
(D) Catholics were a minority during the Tudor era
(E) indulgences offended the aristocracy

Your Answer _____

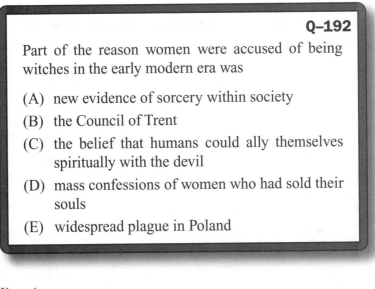

Q–192

Part of the reason women were accused of being witches in the early modern era was

(A) new evidence of sorcery within society
(B) the Council of Trent
(C) the belief that humans could ally themselves spiritually with the devil
(D) mass confessions of women who had sold their souls
(E) widespread plague in Poland

Your Answer _____

Correct Answers

A–191

(A) Unlike the theological and political backdrop to the Reformation in Germany, the English break with Rome had to do with the pope's refusal to grant a divorce between the king and his Spanish queen. Only the pope could grant a royal annulment or divorce, and he would not do so for Henry VIII. This was the backdrop to Henry's decision to separate from the Roman Catholic Church and create a domestic faith based in England under the crown.

A–192

(C) Many common superstitions combined to lead people to fear women as spiritual allies of the devil. The devil and witches were blamed for misfortunes such as crop failure or mental illness. The spirit world was thought to be a tangible part of religious beliefs at this time in history.

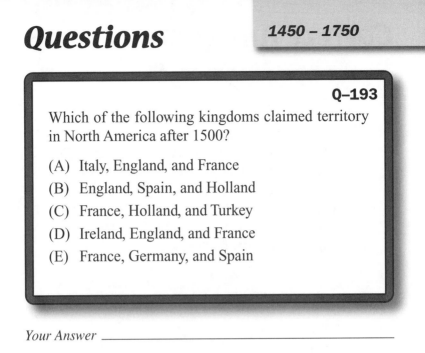

Q–193

Which of the following kingdoms claimed territory in North America after 1500?

(A) Italy, England, and France

(B) England, Spain, and Holland

(C) France, Holland, and Turkey

(D) Ireland, England, and France

(E) France, Germany, and Spain

Your Answer _____

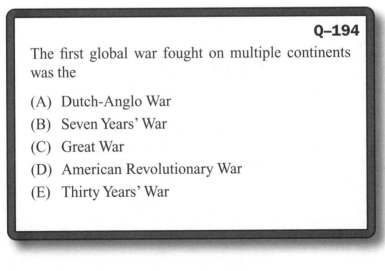

Q–194

The first global war fought on multiple continents was the

(A) Dutch-Anglo War

(B) Seven Years' War

(C) Great War

(D) American Revolutionary War

(E) Thirty Years' War

Your Answer _____

Correct Answers

A–193

(B) The Spanish were the first European kingdom to claim land in North America, but they were soon followed by Britain, Holland, and France. The Spanish maintained their hegemony in Central America, while the French, British, and Dutch fought for control of eastern North America. A series of wars were fought, with the British claiming victory after 1763.

A–194

(B) European rivalry between Britain and France escalated into a global conflict in the 1700s. Control over south Asia and North America was part of the reason for this conflict. The war began in present-day Pennsylvania and spread to Europe and Asia. When it was finished, the British had won important gains in India and the Americas.

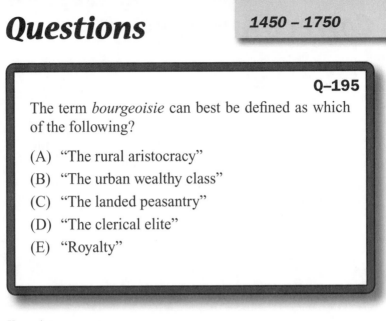

Q–195

The term *bourgeoisie* can best be defined as which of the following?

(A) "The rural aristocracy"

(B) "The urban wealthy class"

(C) "The landed peasantry"

(D) "The clerical elite"

(E) "Royalty"

Your Answer _____

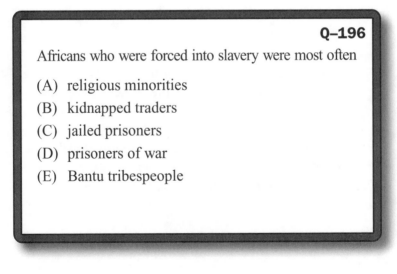

Q–196

Africans who were forced into slavery were most often

(A) religious minorities

(B) kidnapped traders

(C) jailed prisoners

(D) prisoners of war

(E) Bantu tribespeople

Your Answer _____

Correct Answers

A–195

(B) The growing urban merchant class became known as the *bourgeoisie*. An earlier French term for medieval inhabitants of towns, the *bourgeoisie* were neither peasants nor nobility. This class of townspeople was called the merchant/artisan class.

A–196

(D) African tribes often warred with one another, and a common outcome of the fighting was the capture of other tribespeople. When Europeans started offering money for slaves, the capture of other Africans became a feature of the international slave trade. Lucrative relationships were developed between certain coastal African tribes and the European slave traders.

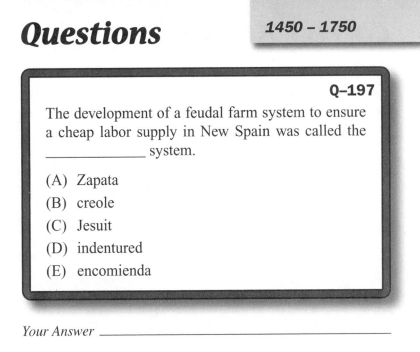

Q–197

The development of a feudal farm system to ensure a cheap labor supply in New Spain was called the _____ system.

(A) Zapata

(B) creole

(C) Jesuit

(D) indentured

(E) encomienda

Your Answer _____

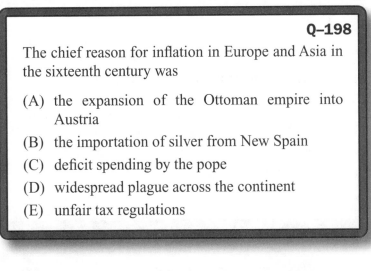

Q–198

The chief reason for inflation in Europe and Asia in the sixteenth century was

(A) the expansion of the Ottoman empire into Austria

(B) the importation of silver from New Spain

(C) deficit spending by the pope

(D) widespread plague across the continent

(E) unfair tax regulations

Your Answer _____

Correct Answers

A–197

(E) The encomienda system was a state-sponsored labor system that gave colonials the power to use natives as de facto slaves. This practice systematized the oppression of Native Americans and left them politically weak and disadvantaged. The privileges of conquest were used by the Spanish to take advantage of the conquered people and make them work for Spain.

A–198

(B) The large quantities of precious metal, particularly silver brought from the New World by the Spanish, had an inflationary impact on the European economy. From Spain to the Ottoman Empire, silver coinage flooded the market, diminishing the value of money. This meant an increase in prices, which is a classic feature of inflation.

 Take Test-Readiness Quiz 2 on CD
(to review questions 100–198)

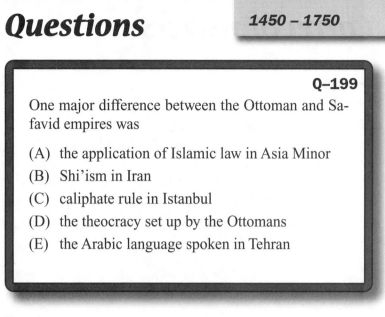

Q–199

One major difference between the Ottoman and Safavid empires was

(A) the application of Islamic law in Asia Minor

(B) Shi'ism in Iran

(C) caliphate rule in Istanbul

(D) the theocracy set up by the Ottomans

(E) the Arabic language spoken in Tehran

Your Answer _____

_____

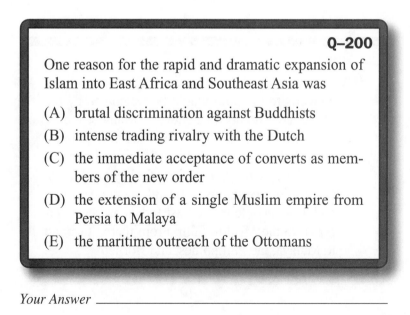

Q–200

One reason for the rapid and dramatic expansion of Islam into East Africa and Southeast Asia was

(A) brutal discrimination against Buddhists

(B) intense trading rivalry with the Dutch

(C) the immediate acceptance of converts as members of the new order

(D) the extension of a single Muslim empire from Persia to Malaya

(E) the maritime outreach of the Ottomans

Your Answer _____

_____

Correct Answers

A–199

(B) The Islamic schism between Sunni and Shia is evident when comparing the Ottoman and the Persian Safavid empires. Shia found its greatest following in the area east of Arabia, in present-day Iraq and Iran. Conflicts between the Turks and Persians from the sixteenth century helped deepen the rift between the two major schools of Islamic tradition.

A–200

(C) As Islam spread to Africa and South Asia, new converts to the faith would be welcomed by the global community of believers. Many seagoing traders were responsible for introducing the practices of Islam to port cities. This solidified the growth of the religion to areas far beyond Arabia. By the fourteenth and fifteenth centuries, more and more people in the East Indies had been exposed to the Muslim faith. From there, it spread to Malaya, the Philippines, and Borneo.

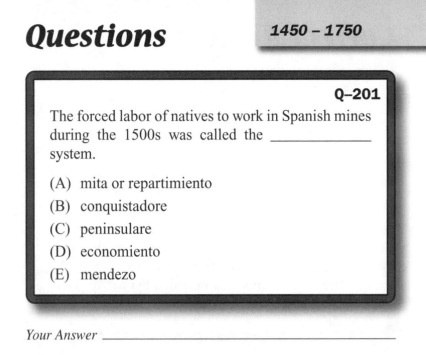

Q–201

The forced labor of natives to work in Spanish mines during the 1500s was called the _____ system.

(A) mita or repartimiento

(B) conquistadore

(C) peninsulare

(D) economiento

(E) mendezo

Your Answer _____

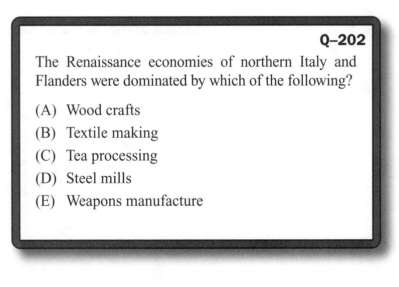

Q–202

The Renaissance economies of northern Italy and Flanders were dominated by which of the following?

(A) Wood crafts

(B) Textile making

(C) Tea processing

(D) Steel mills

(E) Weapons manufacture

Your Answer _____

Correct Answers

A–201

(A) The taking over of Inca mines by the Spanish meant an expansion of operations to extract as much silver and gold from South America as possible. To do this, a forced labor system called the mita was established, where thousands of natives were forced to work for the Spanish. While they might be paid for this labor, the conditions were harsh and many died in the course of this work. It underscored the rigid hierarchy the Spanish imposed in which the natives were treated as underlings and sometimes much like slaves.

A–202

(B) Early modern industry is almost always begun with light manufacture involving textile operations. The Italians and Flemish began to dominate regional markets in the making of cloth and materials made from organic fibers such as wool and cotton. The success of this industry helped spur the development of dynamic economies in southern and northern Europe.

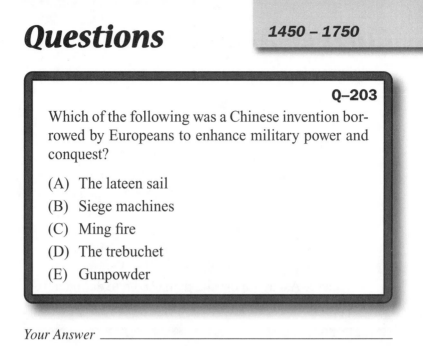

Q–203

Which of the following was a Chinese invention borrowed by Europeans to enhance military power and conquest?

(A) The lateen sail

(B) Siege machines

(C) Ming fire

(D) The trebuchet

(E) Gunpowder

Your Answer _____

_____

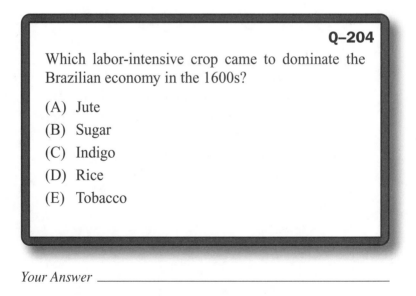

Q–204

Which labor-intensive crop came to dominate the Brazilian economy in the 1600s?

(A) Jute

(B) Sugar

(C) Indigo

(D) Rice

(E) Tobacco

Your Answer _____

_____

Correct Answers

A–203

(E) Discovered by Chinese alchemists over a thousand years ago, gunpowder was an Asian invention that was little developed until Arabs began to use it c. 1280. Western observers were quick to see its potential, and Italian states began to adapt it to medieval warfare. Over time it revolutionized modern warfare as cannon, mortars, and smaller firearms were improved for battle use. By the Age of Discovery, the West had taken the Asian import and then used it to dominate peoples on three continents.

A–204

(B) The European appetite for sugar grew after the discovery of the New World. The tropical regions of Latin America were well suited for growing the cane but it demanded a lot of manual labor to harvest. Brazil was used by Portugal as a plantation colony. Sugar remained the mainstay of the Brazilian economy for 300 years.

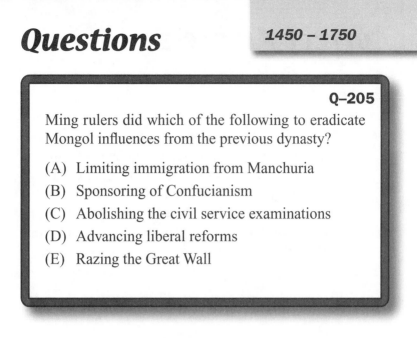

Q–205

Ming rulers did which of the following to eradicate Mongol influences from the previous dynasty?

(A) Limiting immigration from Manchuria
(B) Sponsoring of Confucianism
(C) Abolishing the civil service examinations
(D) Advancing liberal reforms
(E) Razing the Great Wall

Your Answer _____

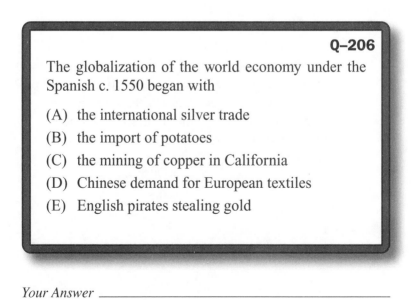

Q–206

The globalization of the world economy under the Spanish c. 1550 began with

(A) the international silver trade
(B) the import of potatoes
(C) the mining of copper in California
(D) Chinese demand for European textiles
(E) English pirates stealing gold

Your Answer _____

Correct Answers

A–205

(B) Ming rulers wished to return China to a pre-Yuan state. The traditional Confucian values all supported the ruling regime in a Chinese context. Imperial academies taught the Confucian philosophy that had framed many previous dynasties. This conservative rule would continue into the twentieth century as the modern era began after 1911.

A–206

(A) With the large output of silver from Mexican and Peruvian mines, the Spanish began to exchange their coinage for goods worldwide. The Chinese especially wished to trade their silks and other wares for Spanish silver. From Europe to Asia, silver became a globally-traded commodity that affected economies in many different regions.

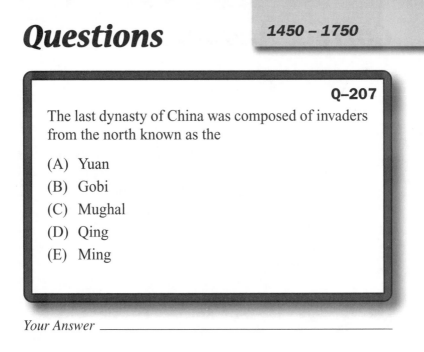

Q–207

The last dynasty of China was composed of invaders from the north known as the

(A) Yuan
(B) Gobi
(C) Mughal
(D) Qing
(E) Ming

Your Answer _____

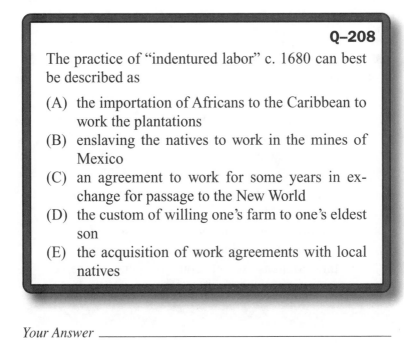

Q–208

The practice of "indentured labor" c. 1680 can best be described as

(A) the importation of Africans to the Caribbean to work the plantations
(B) enslaving the natives to work in the mines of Mexico
(C) an agreement to work for some years in exchange for passage to the New World
(D) the custom of willing one's farm to one's eldest son
(E) the acquisition of work agreements with local natives

Your Answer _____

Correct Answers

A–207

(D) The Ming dynasty began to decline after 1600, and northern invaders came from the northeast to replace them. Like the earlier Mongols, the Qing took up residence in the north and made their capital at Beijing (literally "northern capital"). They dominated the Chinese and also absorbed many of their ways. Ming loyalists continued to oppose them for many generations but with little success.

A–208

(C) The demand for cheap labor in the New World helped create "work for passage" agreements between land owners and poor immigrants. Many farms grew cash crops such as tobacco and cotton, which needed laborers in the fields. The arrangement appealed to many poor Europeans who wanted to make a new life in the Americas but did not have the money to get started. In exchange for a period of work (i.e., seven years), they could aspire to become farmers themselves over time.

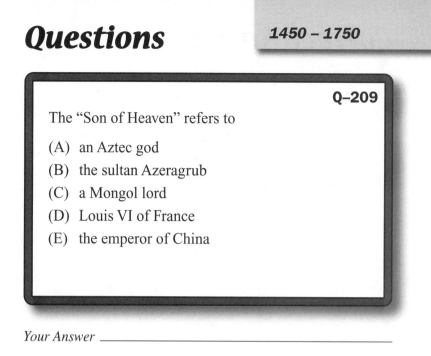

Q–209

The "Son of Heaven" refers to

(A) an Aztec god
(B) the sultan Azeragrub
(C) a Mongol lord
(D) Louis VI of France
(E) the emperor of China

Your Answer _____

_____

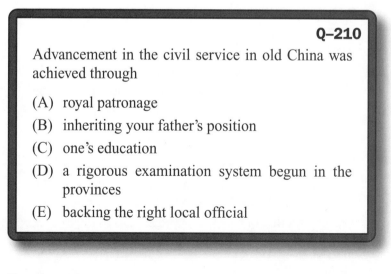

Q–210

Advancement in the civil service in old China was achieved through

(A) royal patronage
(B) inheriting your father's position
(C) one's education
(D) a rigorous examination system begun in the provinces
(E) backing the right local official

Your Answer _____

_____

Correct Answers

A–209

(E) Chinese tradition referred to the emperor as the Son of Heaven. This semidivine title suggested that the emperor reigned at the behest of the gods and his duty was to maintain order in the kingdom. The Qing dynasty institutionalized this tradition and had the emperor live in a walled city within the capital in Beijing. Strict codes of behavior infused court life and few were able to approach the person of the emperor.

A–210

(D) The examination system was long a tradition in dynastic China. Young men of education could vie for positions in the imperial bureaucracy by taking exams in districts that might qualify them for higher positions. Members of the scholar gentry formed the class of the educated functionaries who served the emperor. It allowed for upward advancement and a kind of meritocratic system that selected the smartest men for government work.

Q–211

Which of the following was NOT a common fate for women in traditional China?

(A) Infanticide

(B) Military opportunities

(C) Foot binding

(D) Arranged marriage to another family

(E) Divorce in the case of infertility

Your Answer _____

Q–212

Which of the following was a West African kingdom that controlled trans-Saharan trade routes in the 1400s?

(A) Battutu

(B) Songhai

(C) Kongo

(D) Bantu

(E) Mali

Your Answer _____

Correct Answers

A–211

(B) Although there are rare incidents of female military heroines in Chinese history, warfare was the province of men. Females were seen as underlings subject to the authority of their fathers and husbands. Wives were also subject to their mothers-in-law, who had considerable power over the younger women. Foot binding became more and more standard in the Ming and Qing dynasties and could be a way to make a daughter more attractive to a suitor above one's class.

A–212

(B) A successor to earlier West African trade kingdoms, the Songhai oversaw the exchange of salt and metals. A Muslim regional empire, the Songhai encouraged the expansion of the faith and the building of mosques throughout the kingdom. Its capital at Gao was at an important cultural crossroads and was also an economic center.

Q–213

Which of the following were NOT Chinese goods sought after by the West after 1600?

(A) Lacquerware

(B) Silk

(C) Cotton textiles

(D) Porcelain

(E) Tea

Your Answer _____

_____

Q–214

Which of the following was the central African kingdom that traded with the Portuguese during the early penetration of the West?

(A) Kongo

(B) Zimbabwe

(C) Ghana

(D) Côte d'Ivoire

(E) Zanzibar

Your Answer _____

_____

Correct Answers

A–213

(C) Silk and tea were goods especially desired by Western traders as they penetrated the Asian trading system after Magellan's voyage. The Chinese economy benefited from the influx of silver from North America, which stimulated trade with the Europeans. The silver-based economy also fueled manufacturing.

A–214

(A) Located on the west coast of central Africa, Kongo became an early trading partner with the Portuguese as they ventured down the coast from Europe. Ivory, gold, and slaves became the chief commodities that the Portuguese wanted to purchase. The slave trade flourished after the transplantation of sugar in the New World and especially in Brazil. When the Kongoese resisted the slave raids after a time, the Portuguese simply defeated them and carried on.

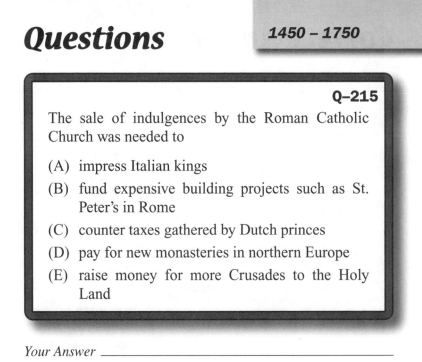

Q–215

The sale of indulgences by the Roman Catholic Church was needed to

(A) impress Italian kings

(B) fund expensive building projects such as St. Peter's in Rome

(C) counter taxes gathered by Dutch princes

(D) pay for new monasteries in northern Europe

(E) raise money for more Crusades to the Holy Land

Your Answer _____

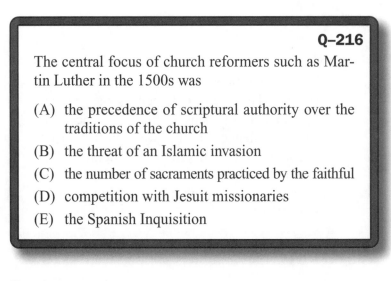

Q–216

The central focus of church reformers such as Martin Luther in the 1500s was

(A) the precedence of scriptural authority over the traditions of the church

(B) the threat of an Islamic invasion

(C) the number of sacraments practiced by the faithful

(D) competition with Jesuit missionaries

(E) the Spanish Inquisition

Your Answer _____

Correct Answers

A–215

(B) The Roman Catholic Church in Italy had grown more powerful and wealthy throughout the Middle Ages. This wealth led to some corruption and exalted lifestyles within the church leadership. It also led to lavish expenditures and grandiose building projects such as the largest basilica ever built. The pope needed considerable income to pay for the huge construction project, so sales of indulgences or church dispensations for the afterlife were encouraged.

A–216

(A) Martin Luther and other reformers objected to Catholic traditions that did not have a basis in scripture. The sale of indulgences was the most objectionable of many Catholic practices that Luther challenged. Luther went on to translate the Bible into German so that all literate believers could read the Word for themselves and not be dependent on Catholic priests to interpret God's Word.

Q-217

Which of the following events ended in regicide in the seventeenth century?

(A) The trial of Galileo

(B) The English Civil War

(C) The Lisbon earthquakes

(D) The War of Spanish Succession

(E) The Ottoman invasion of the Balkans

Your Answer _____

_____

Q-218

Protestantism became dominant in which of the following areas of Europe?

(A) Italy and Ireland

(B) Southern Germany and Austria

(C) France and Spain

(D) Scandinavia and England

(E) Holland and Portugal

Your Answer _____

_____

Correct Answers

A–217

(B) The tension between the king and the Parliament in the 1600s in England led to civil war between 1642 and 1648. Parliament was dominated by the expanding middle class, many of whom were Puritans. They defeated the king and tried him in Parliament. Found guilty of treason and tyrannical rule, Charles I was executed in public in London. The regicide set a precedent in English history for the possible removal of an unjust or even unpopular king.

A–218

(D) Protestantism eventually established itself in northern Europe, which included Scandinavia, Northern Germany, England, and Holland. The Catholic Church retained a majority in France, Italy, Austria, Bavaria, Ireland, and Poland.

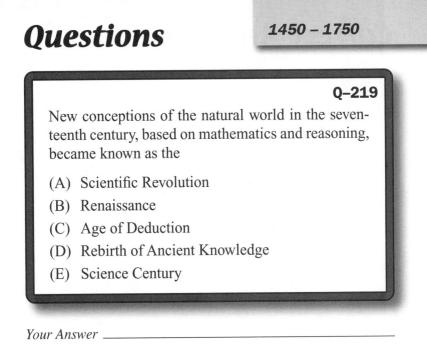

Q–219

New conceptions of the natural world in the seventeenth century, based on mathematics and reasoning, became known as the

(A) Scientific Revolution

(B) Renaissance

(C) Age of Deduction

(D) Rebirth of Ancient Knowledge

(E) Science Century

Your Answer _____

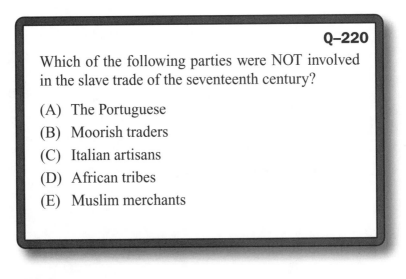

Q–220

Which of the following parties were NOT involved in the slave trade of the seventeenth century?

(A) The Portuguese

(B) Moorish traders

(C) Italian artisans

(D) African tribes

(E) Muslim merchants

Your Answer _____

Correct Answers

A-219

(A) With the rediscovery of ancient texts during the Renaissance, the work of Greco-Roman scientists inspired new observations and calculations with regard to the natural world. Scientists such as Brahe and Galileo built observatories and made breakthroughs in astronomy that surpassed the Greeks of old.

A-220

(C) The slave trade flourished in southwestern Europe, coastal Africa, and the New World in the 1600s. Africans traded slaves with each other, and Muslim caravans took slaves north to be sold in Mediterrean ports. The Portuguese traded for slaves down the west coast of Africa and began to transship them to colonies in the Americas.

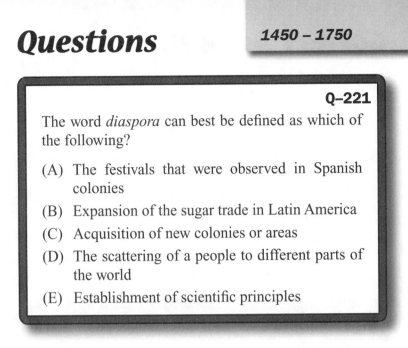

Q–221

The word *diaspora* can best be defined as which of the following?

(A) The festivals that were observed in Spanish colonies

(B) Expansion of the sugar trade in Latin America

(C) Acquisition of new colonies or areas

(D) The scattering of a people to different parts of the world

(E) Establishment of scientific principles

Your Answer _____

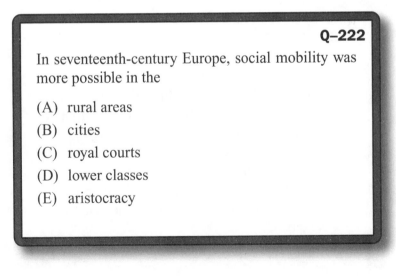

Q–222

In seventeenth-century Europe, social mobility was more possible in the

(A) rural areas

(B) cities

(C) royal courts

(D) lower classes

(E) aristocracy

Your Answer _____

Correct Answers

A–221

(D) At different times in history, certain peoples have dispersed and scattered. This could be the result of conquest and captivity. In the case of Africans during the seventeenth century, tens of thousands of slaves were taken to the Americas to work. This led to a cultural transplantation to the New World, where African language and customs blended with others. New dialects and musical forms sprang up from Argentina to Canada.

A–222

(B) The growth of cities and the merchant classes led to some upward mobility in seventeenth-century Europe. Society was still ordered from top to bottom, with the wealthy landed elites still holding most of the power. But an emerging merchant middle class began to grow in influence, and success in business was a new opportunity for some. The biggest agent of change was the early modern economy, which was centered in the cities.

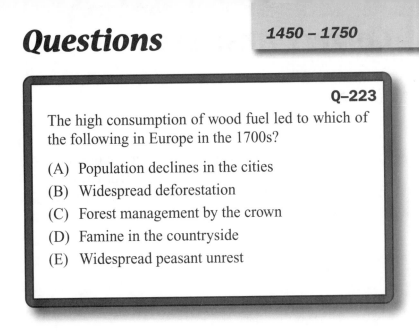

Q–223

The high consumption of wood fuel led to which of the following in Europe in the 1700s?

(A) Population declines in the cities

(B) Widespread deforestation

(C) Forest management by the crown

(D) Famine in the countryside

(E) Widespread peasant unrest

Your Answer _____

_____

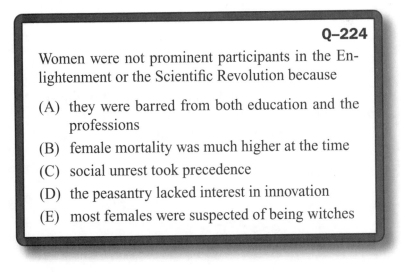

Q–224

Women were not prominent participants in the Enlightenment or the Scientific Revolution because

(A) they were barred from both education and the professions

(B) female mortality was much higher at the time

(C) social unrest took precedence

(D) the peasantry lacked interest in innovation

(E) most females were suspected of being witches

Your Answer _____

_____

Correct Answers

A–223

(B) Both farming and new industries needed fuel, and wood was the most widely used. As populations and families grew, more and more trees were felled and forests were depleted. The once fabled Sherwood Forest was over 10,000 acres and now is less than 700. The rural poor felt the lack of fuel most severely.

A–224

(A) Daughters were not groomed for professional life by their parents. Higher education was dominated by males, and the number of literate women was small. It was a rare wealthy family that would see to the education of a daughter.

Q–225

"Be it enacted by authority of this present Parliament that the King our sovereign lord, his heirs and successors kings of this realm, shall be taken, accepted and reputed the only supreme head in earth of the Church of England called Anglicana Ecclesia . . . ."

The above primary source, dated 1534, has to do with the

(A) king's trial in Parliament

(B) king's obedience to the pope

(C) Reformation in England

(D) war in Ireland

(E) Magna Carta

Your Answer _____

_____

Correct Answers

A–225

(C) The Act of Supremacy in 1534 was a dramatic break between the English crown and the Roman Catholic Church. After being denied a divorce from his Spanish queen, Henry VIII created his own church and placed himself at its head. This power struggle between church and state revealed the growing power of monarchs in Europe, who were able to defy church authority.

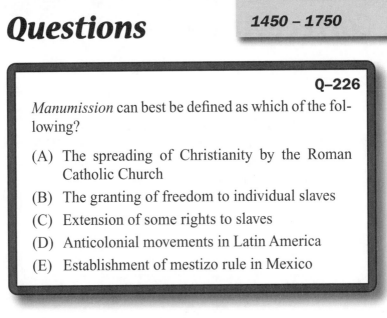

Q–226

Manumission can best be defined as which of the following?

(A) The spreading of Christianity by the Roman Catholic Church

(B) The granting of freedom to individual slaves

(C) Extension of some rights to slaves

(D) Anticolonial movements in Latin America

(E) Establishment of mestizo rule in Mexico

Your Answer _____

_____

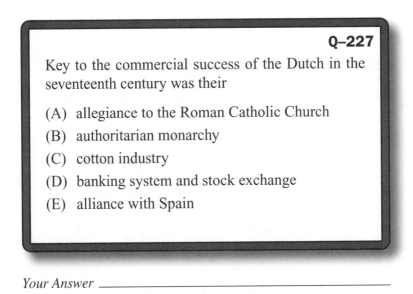

Q–227

Key to the commercial success of the Dutch in the seventeenth century was their

(A) allegiance to the Roman Catholic Church

(B) authoritarian monarchy

(C) cotton industry

(D) banking system and stock exchange

(E) alliance with Spain

Your Answer _____

_____

Correct Answers

A–226

(B) Because slaves were the private property of individuals, it became somewhat common for a person to grant freedom to a given slave. This could also happen at the death of the master, as in the case of George Washington.

A–227

(D) The 1600s have sometimes been called the Dutch century. This small republic became a major economic power in Europe and the world because they developed a sophisticated financial system as well as a robust navy. The Dutch fought with the British over control of Africa and parts of North America. They also colonized parts of Asia and established the Dutch East Indies.

Q–228

Which of the following are NOT components that define a nation?

(A) Financial indexes

(B) History

(C) Language

(D) Religion

(E) Competition with other peoples

Your Answer _____

_____

Q–229

Which of the following explains why Russia lagged behind Western Europe in its development?

(A) The eradication of Islam from Central Asia

(B) Influence of the Ottomans in their affairs

(C) Massive immigration after the Mongol invasion

(D) Poor economic management

(E) Authoritarian rulers and cultural isolation

Your Answer _____

_____

Correct Answers

A–228

(A) Many things come together to define a nation or people. There is shared experience over time and also key cultural components, such as a common language and set of beliefs. Some of the components may be in tension, such as competing variants of a religion or more than one language, but there will be an overarching sense of what it is to be a German, for example, or a Canadian.

A–229

(E) Russia took longer to develop into a nation-state for a number of reasons. Russian monarchs and rulers tended to be heavy-handed and despotic. This gave the Russian people little control over their lives and no practice in governing themselves. Russia also suffered a period of rule by the Mongols, which isolated them culturally from the rest of Europe in the late medieval period. Even rulers like Peter the Great, who wanted Russia to catch up with other kingdoms, was an old-fashioned autocrat who gave no power to others around him.

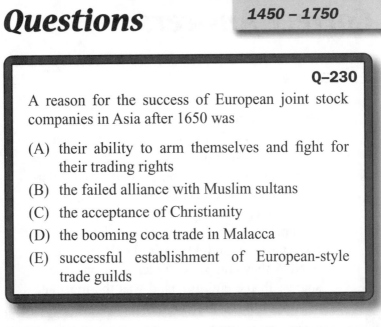

Q–230

A reason for the success of European joint stock companies in Asia after 1650 was

(A) their ability to arm themselves and fight for their trading rights

(B) the failed alliance with Muslim sultans

(C) the acceptance of Christianity

(D) the booming coca trade in Malacca

(E) successful establishment of European-style trade guilds

Your Answer _____

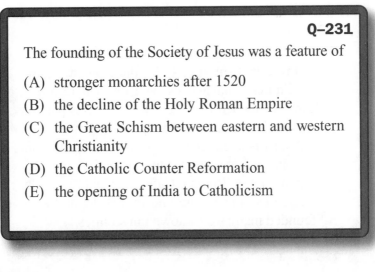

Q–231

The founding of the Society of Jesus was a feature of

(A) stronger monarchies after 1520

(B) the decline of the Holy Roman Empire

(C) the Great Schism between eastern and western Christianity

(D) the Catholic Counter Reformation

(E) the opening of India to Catholicism

Your Answer _____

Correct Answers

A–230

(A) Joint stock companies, which originated in England, Holland, and France, made aggressive inroads into Asia after 1650. These companies enjoyed the support of their monarchies back in Europe but also organized their own military capabilities. When necessary, they fought with local forces who opposed them and also with each other. A series of wars took place in India, the Americas, and Africa in the 1600s and beyond as they competed for territory and market shares. In the end, England was the most successful of the commercial traders.

A–231

(D) After the loss of northern European kingdoms to Protestantism after 1530, the Roman Catholic Church launched its own internal reforms. Loyola founded the Society of Jesus as part of these reforms and this group (also named Jesuits) spearheaded energetic evangelizing both in Europe and abroad. Jesuits opened China and Japan to the Roman Catholic Church, made numerous converts around the world, and also founded many well-known universities.

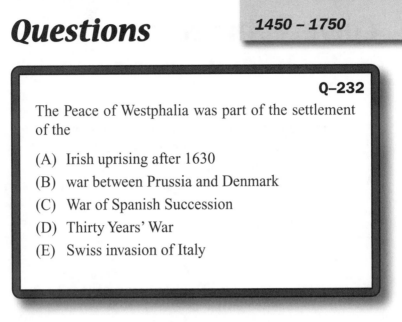

Q–232

The Peace of Westphalia was part of the settlement of the

(A) Irish uprising after 1630

(B) war between Prussia and Denmark

(C) War of Spanish Succession

(D) Thirty Years' War

(E) Swiss invasion of Italy

Your Answer _____

_____

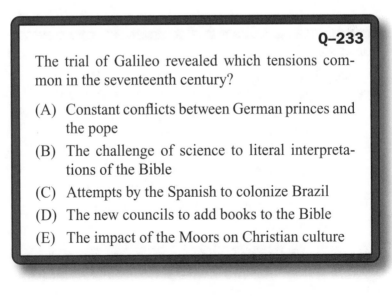

Q–233

The trial of Galileo revealed which tensions common in the seventeenth century?

(A) Constant conflicts between German princes and the pope

(B) The challenge of science to literal interpretations of the Bible

(C) Attempts by the Spanish to colonize Brazil

(D) The new councils to add books to the Bible

(E) The impact of the Moors on Christian culture

Your Answer _____

_____

Correct Answers

A–232

(D) The post-Reformation order in northern Europe was chaotic and violent. Northern Protestant armies fought with Catholic forces for a generation over German territory. The Peace of Westphalia settled the end of the Thirty Years' War and granted certain German states their independence.

A–233

(B) Galileo followed the footsteps of Brahe and suggested an alternative to the geocentric view of the solar system. By suggesting that the sun was the center of our system, he contradicted some orthodox interpretations of Old Testament scripture. Science was forced at that time to conform to traditional church beliefs, and Galileo was put under house arrest for the remainder of his life.

Q–234

The struggle between Parliament and the king of England in the 1600s revealed

(A) vigorous religious turmoil in the aftermath of the Reformation

(B) social unrest between the Welsh and the Scottish

(C) the first movement toward the abolition of slavery

(D) a stronger monarchy in the kingdom

(E) a resurgent influence by the cardinals

Your Answer _____

Q–235

Which of the following empires or kingdoms were NOT expanding in the early 1600s?

(A) Portugal

(B) The Ottoman

(C) The Mughal

(D) The Spanish

(E) The Egyptian

Your Answer _____

Correct Answers

A–234

(A) Religion was the hottest issue in England after the break with Rome under Henry VIII. While Elizabeth had steered a middle course during her reign, the Stuarts after her were not so neutral in regard to the role of the church in England. Economic issues forced a showdown between the king and Parliament and, in the end, war settled the tension when the king was beheaded in London.

A–235

(E) The Portuguese, Spanish, Ottoman Turks, and the Mughals in India were at the apex of their powers in the early seventeenth century. While the Iberians expanded overseas and brought back the wealth of the Americas, the Ottomans expanded into northern Africa and the Middle East. Trade and economic outreach was achieved by all of these powers, but within a hundred years they would all be in decline.

Q–236

The last foreign dynasty to rule China after 1644 was the

(A) Ming dynasty
(B) Han dynasty
(C) Chung dynasty
(D) Qing dynasty
(E) Yuan dynasty

Your Answer _____

Q–237

The concept of "balance of power" found its origin in the period after the

(A) Glorious Revolution
(B) Peace of Westphalia, which sought to keep any one nation from dominating the rest of Europe
(C) death of Suliman the Magnificent
(D) rise of the Papal States
(E) discovery of the Americas by Portugal

Your Answer _____

Correct Answers

A–236

(D) The two foreign dynasties to rule China in the last thousand years were the Yuan or Mongols after 1279 and the Qing or Manchus after 1644. The Qing came from the northeast and overthrew the Ming dynasty. The Qing would rule for centuries, until the republican revolution of 1911.

A–237

(B) After the settlement of the Thirty Years' War at the Peace of Westphalia, agreements among kingdoms attempted to create a balance of power so that no kingdom could become too powerful. Adjustments were made to territories so that some would gain and others would lose influence. A kind of balance was also created between the Catholic south and the Protestant north so that neither branch of Christianity would be dominant.

Q-238

One of the most striking trends after 1500 is the movement of peoples from

(A) Europe to Asia
(B) the New to the Old World
(C) north to south over time
(D) rural to urban societies
(E) the coasts to the hinterland

Your Answer _____

Q-239

Divine right can best be defined as which of the following?

(A) Governments derive their power from the people.
(B) Nations have the right to expand beyond their borders.
(C) Church and state are separate entities.
(D) Parliaments are established by church authority.
(E) Monarchical power is ordained by God.

Your Answer _____

Correct Answers

A–238

(D) After the 1500s, the global trend toward urbanization is impossible to ignore. Population growth and economic activity drew people away from the countryside. Capital cities became not only political centers but also economic ones. Job creation in the cities became a magnet for the rural poor attracted to a different lifestyle.

A–239

(E) In the Age of Absolutism, kings claimed to have authority from God to rule their kingdoms. This was a combining of religious and political dynamics to rationalize the rule of the few over the many. Both church and royalty fostered this belief and preached that to oppose the king was to oppose God. This was challenged in the 1600s as the Enlightenment took hold and new values about the rights of humans began to surface in Europe.

Q–240

Man being born, as has been proved, with a title to perfect freedom and an uncontrolled enjoyment of all the rights and privileges of the law of Nature, equally with any other man, or number of men in the world, hath by nature a power not only to preserve his property—that is, his life, liberty, and estate, against the injuries and attempts of other men. . . .

John Locke, 1689

The above text expressed the philosophy of the period in history known as the

(A) Renaissance

(B) Commercial Revolution

(C) Enlightenment

(D) Great Schism

(E) Industrial Revolution

Your Answer _____

Correct Answers

A–240

(C) The 1600s saw a flowering of new ideas about society and politics. French and British thinkers began to explore the relationship between the people and their government. They considered people to exist in a state of nature, which suggested certain universal rights. Locke was one of the great political philosophers of this time period, now labeled the Enlightenment.

Questions

Q–241

"Liberté, Equalité, Fraternité" was the motto associated with the

(A) Cuban Revolution

(B) nineteenth-century labor movement

(C) Russian Revolution

(D) French Revolution

(E) Commercial Revolution

Your Answer _____

Q–242

The philosophes of the eighteenth century supported which kind of government?

(A) Theocracy

(B) Enlightened despotism

(C) Limited self-rule

(D) Totalitarian dictatorship

(E) Democracy with universal suffrage

Your Answer _____

Correct Answers

A–241

(D) Born out of the Enlightenment philosophies of the eighteenth century, French revolutionaries called for new political freedoms and more equality for the people. New ideas of government and politics developed the belief that rights should be guaranteed to the people. Abstract concepts of liberty and freedom became a part of the political discourse of the eighteenth century.

A–242

(B) Philosophes such as Voltaire preferred an enlightened monarch who had power but would use it for the benefit of the people. Such rulers kept their absolute power over the people but used their power to care for the kingdom and its people. In the ideal, somewhat similar to the idea of Plato's philosopher-king, this ruler would be wise and not behave selfishly or use oppression to control his subjects.

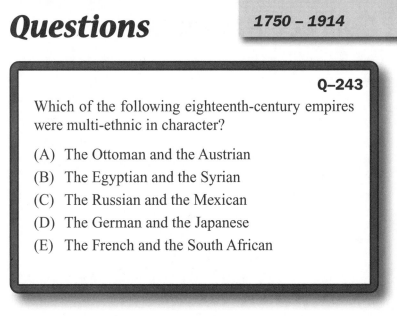

Q–243

Which of the following eighteenth-century empires were multi-ethnic in character?

(A) The Ottoman and the Austrian

(B) The Egyptian and the Syrian

(C) The Russian and the Mexican

(D) The German and the Japanese

(E) The French and the South African

Your Answer _____

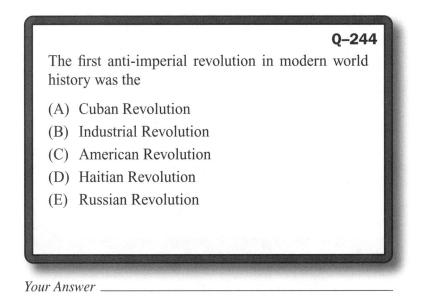

Q–244

The first anti-imperial revolution in modern world history was the

(A) Cuban Revolution

(B) Industrial Revolution

(C) American Revolution

(D) Haitian Revolution

(E) Russian Revolution

Your Answer _____

Correct Answers

A–243

(A) Both the Ottoman and Austrian empires were diverse and multi-ethnic in composition. The Turks ruled over Arabs, Berbers, and Persians, while the Austrians had control over Serbs, Hungarians, Czechs, and others. The difficulty in ruling a large and diverse population would challenge both empires and lead to their eventual dissolution.

A–244

(C) British Americans first wanted to petition the king for more rights, but when relations deteriorated, an independence movement developed that was successful after a long war. The British empire would remain in existence for another century, but American independence was a sign that people could fight back against an imperial oppressor.

Q–245

All the following can be catalysts that lead to political revolution EXCEPT

(A) a large underclass of oppressed people

(B) a corrupt and oblivious regime

(C) an active land reform movement

(D) excessive taxation

(E) a large gap between rich and poor

Your Answer _____

_____

Q–246

A major encouragement to industrialization in the nineteenth century was the development of

(A) labor unions

(B) railroads

(C) reform movements

(D) land grants

(E) transoceanic shipping lanes

Your Answer _____

_____

Correct Answers

A–245

(C) Revolutions are more likely with conservative and uncaring leadership. Often land reform is desperately needed to give the peasantry a stake in their work. Rulers usually resist such reforms and seek to maintain their own power base. Whether one looks at the Chinese or the Cuban revolution, corrupt leadership and a small wealthy elite often give the poor no option but to revolt.

A–246

(B) The ability to move people and goods is an important capability for industrialized nations. During the Industrial Revolution, steam power helped make ships and trains faster and more efficient. Trains replaced canals as a much more effective way to move goods over long distances.

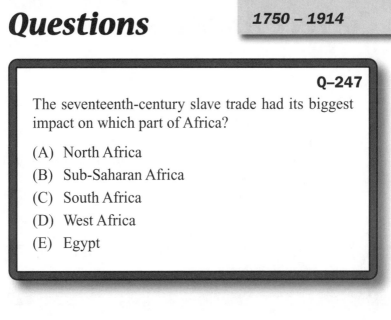

Q–247

The seventeenth-century slave trade had its biggest impact on which part of Africa?

(A) North Africa

(B) Sub-Saharan Africa

(C) South Africa

(D) West Africa

(E) Egypt

Your Answer _____

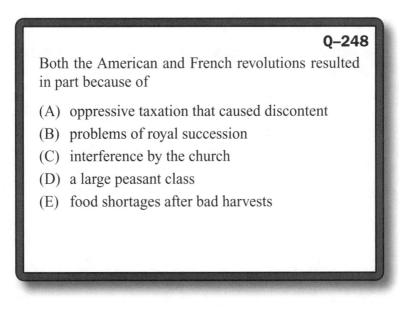

Q–248

Both the American and French revolutions resulted in part because of

(A) oppressive taxation that caused discontent

(B) problems of royal succession

(C) interference by the church

(D) a large peasant class

(E) food shortages after bad harvests

Your Answer _____

Correct Answers

A–247

(D) The slave trade in West Africa was partly a function of geography because this is where the Portuguese arrived in the early years of the Age of Discovery. They established relationships with coastal tribes and began to buy captured Africans from other tribes. As the sugar plantations flourished in the Americas, they needed more and more workers in the cane fields. This caused the slave trade to boom, and more Africans were forced to migrate west.

A–248

(A) The two revolutions had both differences and similarities. In both cases, the king was taxing the people and becoming more unpopular. While French peasants were sometimes taxed at a rate of 70 percent, British Americans disagreed with the mechanisms for raising revenue. Wars caused both governments to revise and raise taxes after 1763.

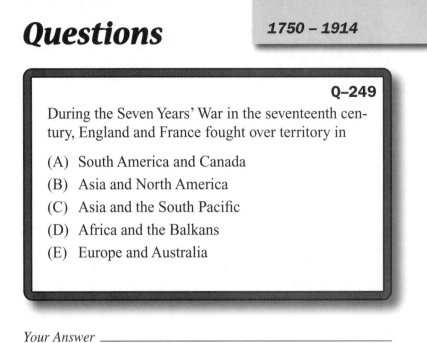

Q-249

During the Seven Years' War in the seventeenth century, England and France fought over territory in

(A) South America and Canada

(B) Asia and North America

(C) Asia and the South Pacific

(D) Africa and the Balkans

(E) Europe and Australia

Your Answer _____

_____

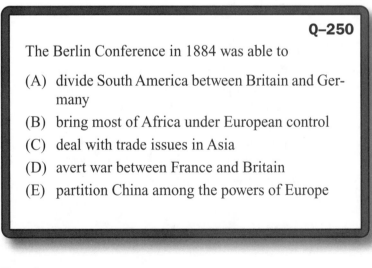

Q-250

The Berlin Conference in 1884 was able to

(A) divide South America between Britain and Germany

(B) bring most of Africa under European control

(C) deal with trade issues in Asia

(D) avert war between France and Britain

(E) partition China among the powers of Europe

Your Answer _____

_____

Correct Answers

A–249

(B) The Seven Years' War (called the French and Indian War in North America) was the first global conflict pitting different European kingdoms against one another. The two major combatants—Britain and France—fought over control of India and also the Ohio River valley in North America. After Britain won, it secured its hold on India and Canada.

A–250

(B) The events of the late 1800s were sometimes called the Scramble for Africa. New powers such as Germany and Italy wanted empires like France and Britain. Germany invited the nations to Berlin to divide the African continent and avoid imperial conflict. All of Africa, except for Ethiopia and Liberia, were taken over by one European power or another.

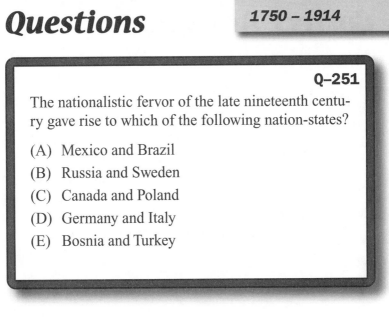

Q-251

The nationalistic fervor of the late nineteenth century gave rise to which of the following nation-states?

(A) Mexico and Brazil

(B) Russia and Sweden

(C) Canada and Poland

(D) Germany and Italy

(E) Bosnia and Turkey

Your Answer _____

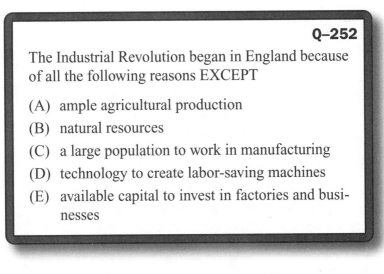

Q-252

The Industrial Revolution began in England because of all the following reasons EXCEPT

(A) ample agricultural production

(B) natural resources

(C) a large population to work in manufacturing

(D) technology to create labor-saving machines

(E) available capital to invest in factories and businesses

Your Answer _____

Correct Answers

A–251

(D) Both revolutionary fervor and nationalistic energy were features of the late 1800s around the world. In Europe, charismatic leaders helped unite both Germany and Italy after 1871. War was often the catalyst of strong patriotic and nationalistic feelings among the people. In Asia, Chinese and Japanese nationalists also urged their people to unite and create modern nation-states.

A–252

(A) The transition from an agricultural-based economy to one based on manufacturing was a key feature of modern industrialization. England was blessed with coal and iron deposits and a growing population. Its government also encouraged business and investment. First, machines were powered by water but when the steam engine was built, steam became the standard means of producing mechanical energy.

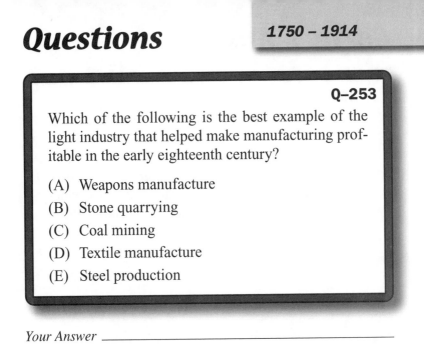

Q–253

Which of the following is the best example of the light industry that helped make manufacturing profitable in the early eighteenth century?

(A) Weapons manufacture

(B) Stone quarrying

(C) Coal mining

(D) Textile manufacture

(E) Steel production

Your Answer _____

_____

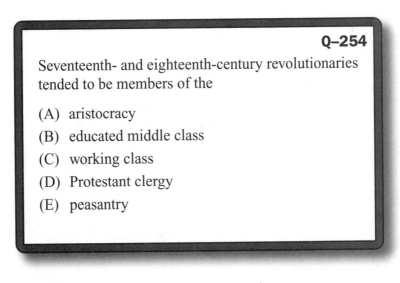

Q–254

Seventeenth- and eighteenth-century revolutionaries tended to be members of the

(A) aristocracy

(B) educated middle class

(C) working class

(D) Protestant clergy

(E) peasantry

Your Answer _____

_____

Correct Answers

A–253

(D) Textile manufacture required less investment and technology to start. Steam-driven looms helped make England and later the United States large-scale producers of cloth goods. Countries that have transitioned from agriculture to manufacturing usually find success in making cheap textile goods and then move up to heavier manufacturing, such as steel production.

A–254

(B) From John Adams to Karl Marx, revolutionaries tended to be educated members of the middle class. Those who led the French, American, and Russian revolutions were well educated and had access to the new ideologies of their time. While the working class was the most oppressed, it was the middle class intelligentsia that wrote about the coming changes and made them happen.

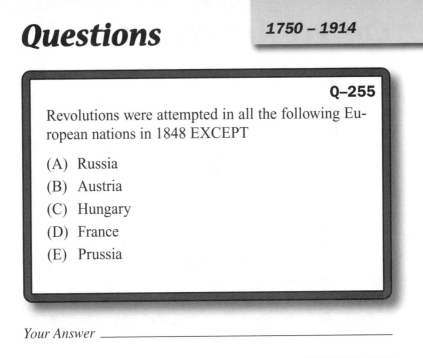

Q–255

Revolutions were attempted in all the following European nations in 1848 EXCEPT

(A) Russia

(B) Austria

(C) Hungary

(D) France

(E) Prussia

Your Answer _____

_____

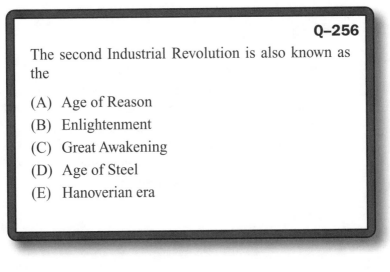

Q–256

The second Industrial Revolution is also known as the

(A) Age of Reason

(B) Enlightenment

(C) Great Awakening

(D) Age of Steel

(E) Hanoverian era

Your Answer _____

_____

Correct Answers

A–255

(A) Revolutions across Europe were inspired by post-Enlightenment liberalism. A belief in more power for the people gave rise to movements that fought for workers' rights and liberal reforms. Such thinking had not made inroads in Russia, where a powerful monarch, called the tsar, ruled. Most of these revolutions did not succeed, but the ideas that stood behind them did produce some changes in government and business.

A–256

(D) The earlier phase of industrialization had to do with steam power and light manufacture. As the 1800s continued, new materials were being produced that changed buildings and engineering. Steel became the material that allowed for taller and taller buildings. It also transformed shipping. Larger military vessels made of steel replaced older wooden sailing ships.

Q–257

What was an impact on women as the West industrialized in the nineteenth century?

(A) More women became poor as prices of goods rose.

(B) More women stayed home as men became wage earners.

(C) The upper class diminished.

(D) There were fewer middle-class women.

(E) Many women rejected reform movements.

Your Answer _____

Q–258

The British empire consisted of all of the following colonies EXCEPT

(A) India

(B) Kenya

(C) South Africa

(D) Brazil

(E) Singapore

Your Answer _____

Correct Answers

A–257

(B) Men who came from the country to work in factories became the breadwinners of the family. This meant that more women typically stayed home to manage the family. As the middle class grew, women saw their roles change. Most women remained in the home, while a few were engaged in professions such as nursing or teaching.

A–258

(D) England colonized many different parts of Africa, including Kenya and South Africa. India, Singapore, Canada, and Jamaica were also part of the British empire. Brazil was a Portuguese colony until its independence in 1822.

Questions

Q–259

During the Qing dynasty, Korea was turned into a

(A) province of China
(B) vassal state
(C) colony of Japan
(D) new kingdom
(E) socialist state

Your Answer _____

Q–260

The decline of the Qing dynasty was demonstrated in the nineteenth century by their defeat by the

(A) Siamese in 1876.
(B) Vietnamese
(C) United States in the Korean War
(D) Germans in the siege of Beijing
(E) British in the Opium War

Your Answer _____

Correct Answers

A–259

(B) Korea is a peninsula extending from Manchuria in East Asia. The Manchus made Korea a vassal state, meaning that it was subservient to them. Koreans paid tribute, or special fees, to the Manchus as a demonstration of their acknowledged dependence.

A–260

(E) The dispute over the opium trade in the 1830s led to two wars in the nineteenth century between Manchu China and Great Britain. Both wars were quick and one-sided because China was no match for British naval power. Treaties were created that made China more commercially open to the West. China also was forced to cede territory to Britain and other Western powers.

Q–261

The creation of a new African state in the 1880s led by the messianic Mahdi in Sudan revealed

(A) Islamic resistance to the intrusion of the West

(B) acceptance by the British of home rule

(C) that Egypt was close to achieving independence

(D) the decline of Islam in north Africa

(E) the failure of missionaries to win converts

Your Answer _____

_____

Q–262

Nothing the sovereign representative can do to a subject, . . . can properly be called injustice or injury.

—Thomas Hobbes

The above quote was used to uphold the institution of

(A) marriage in England

(B) absolute monarchy in Europe

(C) the military in France

(D) the church in Europe

(E) the university in Germany

Your Answer _____

_____

Correct Answers

A–261

(A) Throughout the nineteenth century, various Muslim leaders were active in North Africa in creating Islamic nation-states. Some historians believe this revealed an insecurity as the Christian West made its power known in the region. Egypt was reduced to a British protectorate, and Libya was taken over by the Italians. Africans banded together in different locales and fought small holy wars against the colonizers from Europe. The Mahdi in Sudan was successful at first in defeating the British, but a powerful army defeated him in 1898.

A–262

(B) In his book *Leviathan*, Hobbes justified the rule of kings over their people. His defense of absolute monarchy suggested that royalty gave order to society and the state. While the king should consider the wishes of the people, Hobbes believed that monarchy was the only system to lend stability when kings were attuned to the nation.

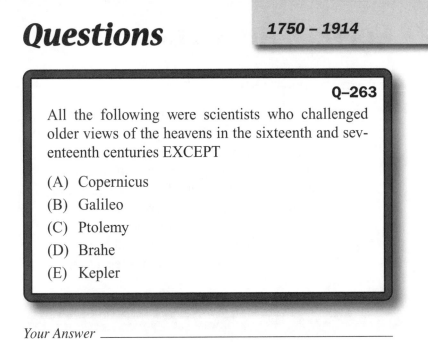

Q–263

All the following were scientists who challenged older views of the heavens in the sixteenth and seventeenth centuries EXCEPT

(A) Copernicus

(B) Galileo

(C) Ptolemy

(D) Brahe

(E) Kepler

Your Answer _____

_____

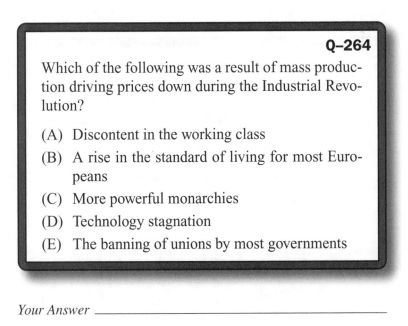

Q–264

Which of the following was a result of mass production driving prices down during the Industrial Revolution?

(A) Discontent in the working class

(B) A rise in the standard of living for most Europeans

(C) More powerful monarchies

(D) Technology stagnation

(E) The banning of unions by most governments

Your Answer _____

_____

Correct Answers

A–263

(C) The 1500s and 1600s were a time of reexamining the heavens and reconsidering the solar system we live in. Ptolemy was the ancient astronomer who first suggested a geocentric universe where the earth was the center of the planetary system. Early modern astronomers, such as Brahe and Galileo, began to question the earlier views of an earth-centered system and proposed a solar-based configuration based on their observations.

A–264

(B) As more and more people came to urban areas to work, factories were able to increase production. This drove prices down as goods flooded the market. A positive outcome was the ability of the working class to buy more. This led to a slow increase in living standards over time.

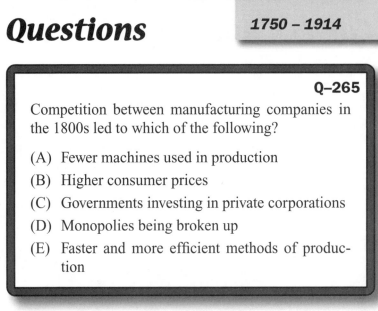

Q–265

Competition between manufacturing companies in the 1800s led to which of the following?

(A) Fewer machines used in production

(B) Higher consumer prices

(C) Governments investing in private corporations

(D) Monopolies being broken up

(E) Faster and more efficient methods of production

Your Answer _____

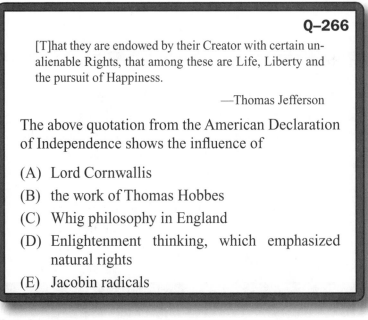

Q–266

[T]hat they are endowed by their Creator with certain unalienable Rights, that among these are Life, Liberty and the pursuit of Happiness.

—Thomas Jefferson

The above quotation from the American Declaration of Independence shows the influence of

(A) Lord Cornwallis

(B) the work of Thomas Hobbes

(C) Whig philosophy in England

(D) Enlightenment thinking, which emphasized natural rights

(E) Jacobin radicals

Your Answer _____

Correct Answers

A–265

(E) Companies competed for market share and had to become more efficient in their production methods. Profits had to be shaved so savings in personnel and technology had to be realized. More sophisticated industrial processes developed to create more production for less money.

A–266

(D) Thomas Jefferson and other American revolutionaries were influenced by Enlightenment thinkers who stressed the natural rights of the people. Enlightenment theorists believed that God was a distant force who had given rights to humankind and it was up to humans to assert these rights. Liberty was a key theme because freedom was seen as a natural state for humans.

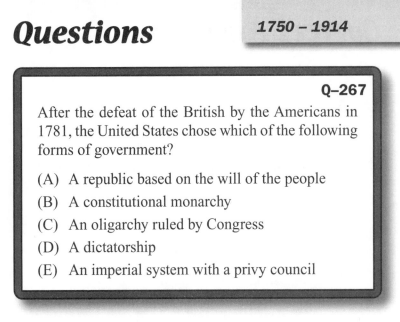

Q–267

After the defeat of the British by the Americans in 1781, the United States chose which of the following forms of government?

(A) A republic based on the will of the people

(B) A constitutional monarchy

(C) An oligarchy ruled by Congress

(D) A dictatorship

(E) An imperial system with a privy council

Your Answer _____

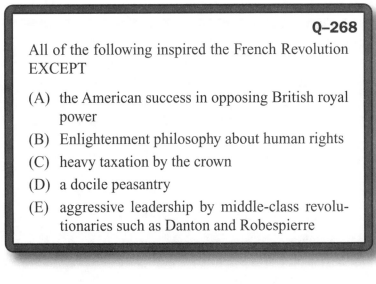

Q–268

All of the following inspired the French Revolution EXCEPT

(A) the American success in opposing British royal power

(B) Enlightenment philosophy about human rights

(C) heavy taxation by the crown

(D) a docile peasantry

(E) aggressive leadership by middle-class revolutionaries such as Danton and Robespierre

Your Answer _____

Correct Answers

A–267

(A) The Americans were deeply influenced by the Enlightenment thinkers who preached the rights of the people. Since the Renaissance rediscovery of Greek and Roman culture, it was natural for the United States to adopt a democratic republic in which the people ruled themselves.

A–268

(D) The French Revolution followed quickly in the aftermath of the American Revolution. Both struggles were inspired by new ideas about republican government and equality as a universal right. The oppression of the inept crown also aggravated the situation and turned the masses against the monarchy.

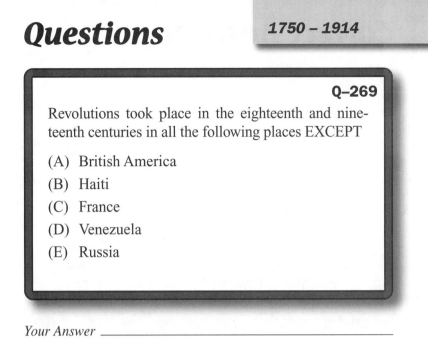

Q–269

Revolutions took place in the eighteenth and nineteenth centuries in all the following places EXCEPT

(A) British America

(B) Haiti

(C) France

(D) Venezuela

(E) Russia

Your Answer _____

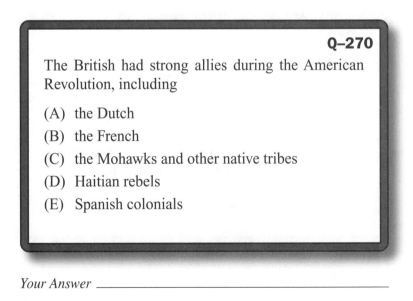

Q–270

The British had strong allies during the American Revolution, including

(A) the Dutch

(B) the French

(C) the Mohawks and other native tribes

(D) Haitian rebels

(E) Spanish colonials

Your Answer _____

Correct Answers

A–269

(E) Often known as the Age of Revolutions, the period from 1770 to 1850 was full of tumult and unrest. From the shots at Concord in Massachusetts to the uprisings in Europe in 1848, there were successful and unsuccessful uprisings in this era. Liberalism was on the move and sought democratic reforms in many parts of the Western world. Russia remained apart from these changes and rather undeveloped compared to other parts of Europe and the Americas.

A–270

(C) The British cultivated their alliances with certain native tribes since before the French and Indian War. During the Revolution, some tribes, such as the Mohawks, fought along the frontier and attacked American settlements. The fear of native attacks was a strong part of British war aims calculated to bring the colonists to the peace table.

Questions

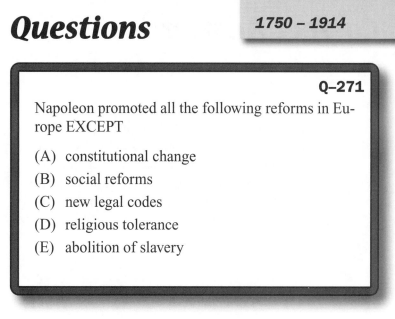

Q–271

Napoleon promoted all the following reforms in Europe EXCEPT

(A) constitutional change

(B) social reforms

(C) new legal codes

(D) religious tolerance

(E) abolition of slavery

Your Answer _____

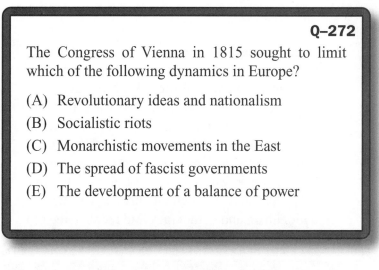

Q–272

The Congress of Vienna in 1815 sought to limit which of the following dynamics in Europe?

(A) Revolutionary ideas and nationalism

(B) Socialistic riots

(C) Monarchistic movements in the East

(D) The spread of fascist governments

(E) The development of a balance of power

Your Answer _____

Correct Answers

A–271

(E) Napoleon was the heir to the French Revolution and promoted many of the Enlightenment ideals from that era. He promoted religious freedom, created a new legal system based on egalitarian ideals, and gave more rights to all adult men. He did not advance the cause of abolition directly; that came later in the nineteenth century.

A–272

(A) The Congress of Vienna was a political reaction to the French successes after their revolution and the wars that followed. With the defeat of Napoleon, Austria, Britain, and Russia sought to create a new balance of power that would be conservative and monarchistic. The French Revolution had inspired liberal democratic movements in various parts of Europe. The conservative interests sought to discourage patriotic nationalism and democracy and recreate the old order before Napoleon came to power.

Q–273

Which of the following Latin American colonies became the first to declare independence?

(A) Brazil

(B) Mexico

(C) Haiti

(D) Cuba

(E) Panama

Your Answer _____

_____

Q–274

Which of the following is the most important cause of independence movements in Latin America in the 1800s?

(A) Successful revolutions in Russia

(B) Dynamic leadership from Sebastian Gomez

(C) War between England and France

(D) Napoleonic invasions that destabilized Europe

(E) Writings by Estavez Omerte

Your Answer _____

_____

Correct Answers

A–273

(C) Haiti declared its independence in 1803 after a successful slave revolt. Led by the charismatic Toussaint L'Ouverture, Haiti was able to achieve its freedom for a time in the early nineteenth century. Other colonies heard of this uprising and became more insecure about their ability to handle large-scale slave uprisings.

A–274

(D) Latin American nationalists heard of the conflict in Europe after 1800 when France began to dominate Spain and other parts of Europe. Once Spain was weakened, its empire began to fall apart. Independence movements went into action in Venezuela and other parts of the Spanish empire.

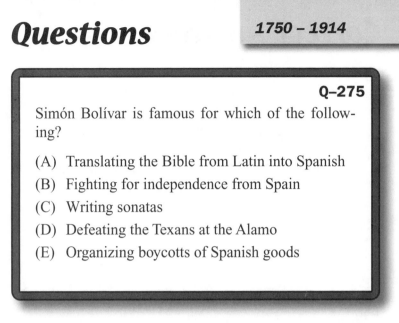

Q–275

Simón Bolívar is famous for which of the following?

(A) Translating the Bible from Latin into Spanish

(B) Fighting for independence from Spain

(C) Writing sonatas

(D) Defeating the Texans at the Alamo

(E) Organizing boycotts of Spanish goods

Your Answer _____

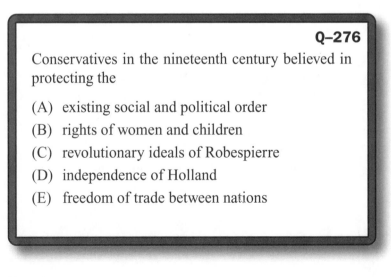

Q–276

Conservatives in the nineteenth century believed in protecting the

(A) existing social and political order

(B) rights of women and children

(C) revolutionary ideals of Robespierre

(D) independence of Holland

(E) freedom of trade between nations

Your Answer _____

Correct Answers

A–275

(B) Simón Bolívar is known as the father of Latin American independence. Called the "liberator" by many, he fought a series of military campaigns to create new nations such as Colombia, Venezuela, Peru, and Bolivia.

A–276

(A) Conservatives in the nineteenth century began to develop an alternative to the revolutionary ideals of the American and French revolutions. They believed that change was natural over time but should not be revolutionary in nature. They worked to preserve the political and social status quo because they were generally averse to change.

Q–277

The term *division of labor* in manufacturing means the

(A) creation of specialized tasks on the factory floor
(B) establishment of union organizations
(C) worker makes the product entirely
(D) making of more layers of management in a company
(E) labor is divided into different factory shifts

Your Answer _____

_____

Q–278

Mass manufacturing of machines became more efficient with the use of

(A) plastic presses
(B) cast iron parts
(C) handmade steel parts
(D) iron smelting
(E) interchangeable parts

Your Answer _____

_____

Correct Answers

A–277

(A) As industrialization became more complex, labor needed to become more specialized. Workers would learn one task in the manufacturing process and do only that task. It could be attaching the wheels to a car or polishing a glass piece on a truck. This created more efficiency, but it also made work more rote and repetitive.

A–278

(E) Interchangeable parts meant that many phases of making a device could be standardized. The fewer the parts, the more simple the machine, and the easier it was to clean and maintain. Repair was also made easier. This was true of automobiles, such as the Ford Model T, and the Colt revolver.

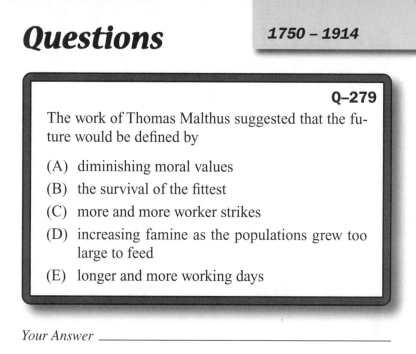

Q–279

The work of Thomas Malthus suggested that the future would be defined by

(A) diminishing moral values

(B) the survival of the fittest

(C) more and more worker strikes

(D) increasing famine as the populations grew too large to feed

(E) longer and more working days

Your Answer _____

_____

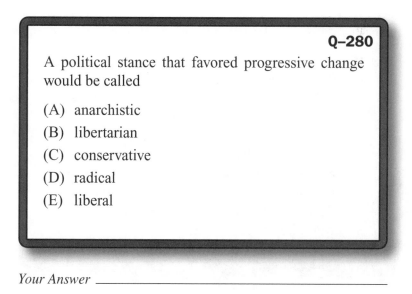

Q–280

A political stance that favored progressive change would be called

(A) anarchistic

(B) libertarian

(C) conservative

(D) radical

(E) liberal

Your Answer _____

_____

Correct Answers

A–279

(D) Malthus believed that growing populations would result in the food supply being unable to sustain so many people. This pessimistic forecast did not take into consideration higher yields in agriculture over time as farming became more efficient. Still, Malthus is one of the early demographers who considered the growth of populations in the modern era.

A–280

(E) In the 1800s liberal and conservative political thinking emerged to separate parties and candidates from one another. Some like Jefferson favored change and believed in revolution when the circumstances called for it. Others like Burke in England saw revolution as dangerous and sought to protect the way things were. Progressive change is the end goal of the liberal, who wants to work within the system to see the world improve.

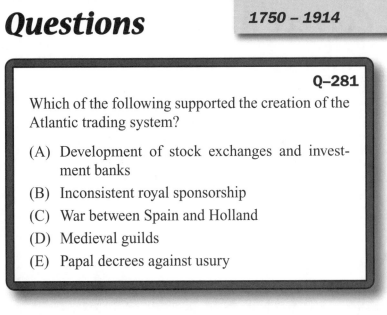

Q–281

Which of the following supported the creation of the Atlantic trading system?

(A) Development of stock exchanges and investment banks

(B) Inconsistent royal sponsorship

(C) War between Spain and Holland

(D) Medieval guilds

(E) Papal decrees against usury

Your Answer _____

_____

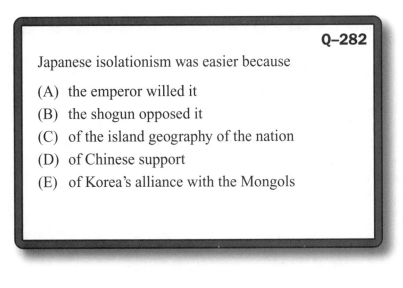

Q–282

Japanese isolationism was easier because

(A) the emperor willed it

(B) the shogun opposed it

(C) of the island geography of the nation

(D) of Chinese support

(E) of Korea's alliance with the Mongols

Your Answer _____

_____

Correct Answers

A-281

(A) Overseas colonization required money which came from royal treasuries or private investors. Modern banking in London and Amsterdam made funds available to investors who wanted to back foreign ventures. Companies sold stock to people who wanted to share the risk and reward of any profits from colonial business.

A-282

(C) Japan evolved over the centuries as a unique and isolated culture in East Asia. Being detached from the Asian mainland meant that Japan was separated from the rest of Asia and was also protected from invasion. After Europeans arrived to trade and offer their religion to Japan, the shogun sealed off the Japanese islands from the outside world.

Q–283

Which of the following resulted from the rapid population increase in Qing China?

(A) Increased military influence in Asia

(B) Degradation of the environment

(C) Greater yields in agriculture

(D) Better roads and transportation infrastructure

(E) A decrease in urban crime

Your Answer _____

_____

Q–284

New nineteenth-century Latin American nations were born out of

(A) regional tensions and rivalries that led to political fragmentation

(B) royal attempts to control New Spain

(C) attempts by the United States to control the Caribbean

(D) conservative nationalist movements

(E) slave revolts across the hemisphere

Your Answer _____

_____

Correct Answers

A–283

(B) With the population topping 300 million people in China in the late 1700s, there were numerous environmental strains in East Asia. People needed more fuel, and deforestation led to erosion and the silting of river ways. Flooding increased, and famine became more common over time.

A–284

(A) After Mexico separated from Spain in the 1820s, resulting power vacuums led to local control and eventual independence. The nations of Honduras, Nicaragua, and others resulted. In the end, dozens of new countries grew out of the old Spanish empire in the New World.

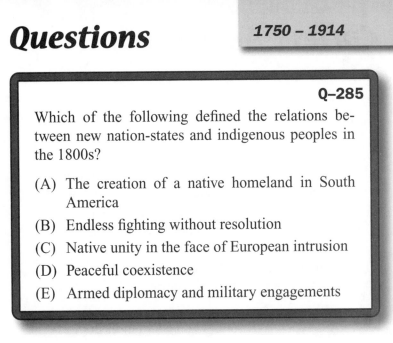

Q–285

Which of the following defined the relations between new nation-states and indigenous peoples in the 1800s?

(A) The creation of a native homeland in South America

(B) Endless fighting without resolution

(C) Native unity in the face of European intrusion

(D) Peaceful coexistence

(E) Armed diplomacy and military engagements

Your Answer _____

_____

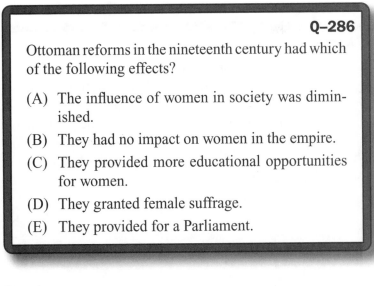

Q–286

Ottoman reforms in the nineteenth century had which of the following effects?

(A) The influence of women in society was diminished.

(B) They had no impact on women in the empire.

(C) They provided more educational opportunities for women.

(D) They granted female suffrage.

(E) They provided for a Parliament.

Your Answer _____

_____

Correct Answers

A–285

(E) From Australia to South Africa, native peoples came into conflict with colonial Westerners who sought to take land and dominate the people there. New nation-states used military might and treaty agreements to subdue native people; when violence broke out, they used military force to put rebellion down. Some alliances between natives resulted, but they were ineffective in resisting the West as it populated African, Asian, and Oceanic territories.

A–286

(A) Ottoman reforms in the latter part of the empire's history further marginalized women in society. All rights were granted only to men. At no time were women participants in the political dialogue in Ottoman Turkey. Matters of clothing and behavior for women remained unchanged into the twentieth century.

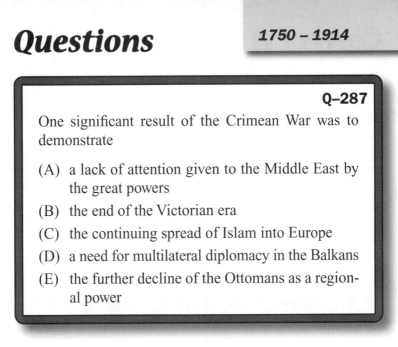

Q–287

One significant result of the Crimean War was to demonstrate

(A) a lack of attention given to the Middle East by the great powers

(B) the end of the Victorian era

(C) the continuing spread of Islam into Europe

(D) a need for multilateral diplomacy in the Balkans

(E) the further decline of the Ottomans as a regional power

Your Answer _____

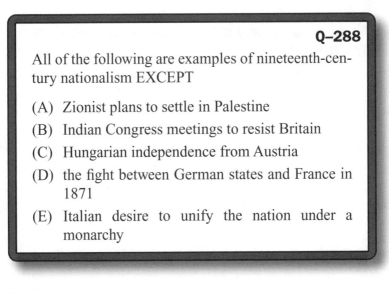

Q–288

All of the following are examples of nineteenth-century nationalism EXCEPT

(A) Zionist plans to settle in Palestine

(B) Indian Congress meetings to resist Britain

(C) Hungarian independence from Austria

(D) the fight between German states and France in 1871

(E) Italian desire to unify the nation under a monarchy

Your Answer _____

Correct Answers

A–287

(E) The so-called eastern question was a way to describe the complex rivalry between a declining Ottoman empire and Russia's desire for more territory in the Balkans. The British and French supported the Ottomans against Russia to maintain a kind of balance and stability in the region. In any case, it showed that the Ottomans were vulnerable to Russian expansion in the region.

A–288

(C) Many expressions of nationalism are evident after the defeat of Napoleon. Some Jewish nationalists began to promote a homeland in the Middle East. Some colonial subjects began to agitate for more home rule under the British. Nations such as Italy and Germany came into being through military campaigns that united the people behind the nationalists.

Q–289

The end goal of Marxist socialism was the creation of

(A) a single-party dictatorship

(B) a classless society

(C) many worker councils in urban areas

(D) a partnership between capitalists and the workers

(E) agricultural collectives

Your Answer _____

_____

Q–290

All of the following are features of Marxist theory EXCEPT

(A) class struggle

(B) capitalistic benefits

(C) proletarian overthrow of the moneyed interests

(D) bourgeoisie exploitation of the workers

(E) international unity of all workers

Your Answer _____

_____

Correct Answers

A–289

(B) Some nineteenth-century socialists were more idealistic than others, but Marx set forth a goal of the classless society. This was to be achieved after the overthrow of capitalism. The means of production were then supposed to be in the hands of the workers. The workers would then create a new order in which goods were shared among the population according to people's needs.

A–290

(B) Marx wrote of the predicted overthrow of capitalism by the workers. He saw the bourgeoisie as the moneyed interests who used the workers and took the profits. Capitalism is the great evil in the eyes of Marx. He saw all history in terms of class struggle, where the poor were exploited by the rich. His theories formed the basis for later socialistic/communistic movements in Russia and China.

Q–291

One of the most profitable cash crops in early modern times was

(A) flax

(B) rice

(C) cotton

(D) sugar

(E) indigo

Your Answer _____

Q–292

All of the following were tactics used by slaves in resisting their masters EXCEPT

(A) work slowdowns

(B) organized protest marches

(C) sabotage of plantation equipment

(D) running away

(E) armed insurrection

Your Answer _____

Correct Answers

A–291

(D) Demand for sugar grew dramatically as Europeans learned to love the sweet additive. Plantations were created in the tropics to produce more sugar for the world market. These plantations relied on slave labor, which helped keep the plantations' products cheap and competitive. White Europeans managed the plantations and slaves did the repetitive, laborious field work.

A–292

(B) Slaves sought their freedom in various ways. Some escaped to remote regions or to other countries. Many resisted passively by working more slowly. Occasionally slaves would revolt and kill their masters, such as in Haiti and the United States. There were no organized protests because blacks had no opportunity to organize themselves beyond any one farm or plantation.

Q–293

Which of the following was a factor in advancing the cause of the abolition of slavery in Europe and the Americas?

(A) Spain abolished slavery in 1720.

(B) Slave rebellions occurred across the Americas.

(C) Business interests found that slavery was immoral.

(D) Wars disrupted trade around the world.

(E) Books and memoirs about slavery were widely publicized.

Your Answer _____

Q–294

The term *ideology* can best be defined as which of the following?

(A) New religious movements

(B) A coherent vision of human society proposing a social and political order

(C) Viewing humans as part of the animal world

(D) The promotion of monarchy as the best political system

(E) A list of ideas promoting social disorder

Your Answer _____

Correct Answers

A–293

(E) Many different factors helped to end slavery in the nineteenth century. One important influence was the printed word in Europe and America. Slaves who had run away to gain their freedom wrote their life stories, and many people learned about the inhuman conditions that Africans endured. Authors such as Harriet Beecher Stowe wrote novels that showed slaves in a human light. These books persuaded many to work for the abolition of slavery.

A–294

(B) The early modern era created new ways of imagining political and social systems. The concepts of liberalism and conservatism were two ideologies that became part of the political dialogue of the 1800s. Various -*isms* were developed as economic and political thinking evolved. New concepts such as human rights contributed to many of the great debates in the Western world.

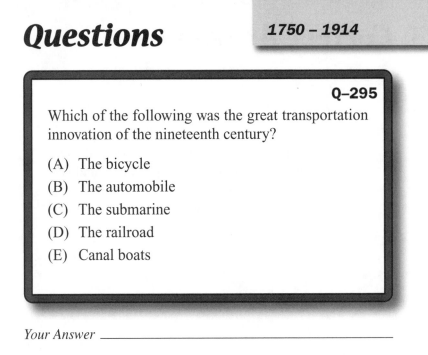

Q–295

Which of the following was the great transportation innovation of the nineteenth century?

(A) The bicycle

(B) The automobile

(C) The submarine

(D) The railroad

(E) Canal boats

Your Answer _____

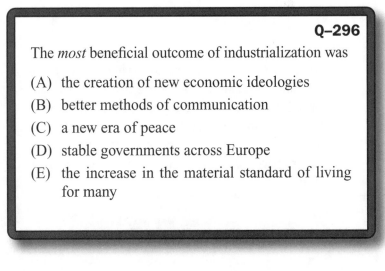

Q–296

The *most* beneficial outcome of industrialization was

(A) the creation of new economic ideologies

(B) better methods of communication

(C) a new era of peace

(D) stable governments across Europe

(E) the increase in the material standard of living for many

Your Answer _____

Correct Answers

A–295

(D) The automobile was invented in the late nineteenth century, but it was the railroad that proved to be the great transportation system of the era. First built in Britain, this new people- and cargo-mover was soon seen in different parts of the world. Wherever Europeans created colonies, they built railroads to connect cities.

A–296

(E) Industrialization had many outcomes but over time, it did produce more goods at cheaper rates for many. Middle-class people could afford new products that made their lives easier. Travel was faster and affordable for many. Simple things such as indoor plumbing contributed greatly to improved comfort and a higher standard of living.

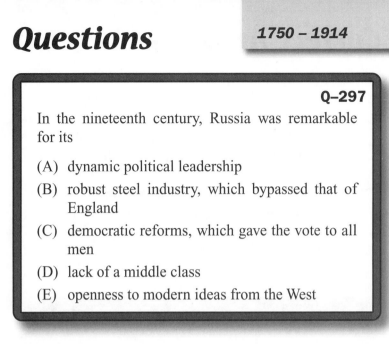

Q–297

In the nineteenth century, Russia was remarkable for its

(A) dynamic political leadership

(B) robust steel industry, which bypassed that of England

(C) democratic reforms, which gave the vote to all men

(D) lack of a middle class

(E) openness to modern ideas from the West

Your Answer _____

_____

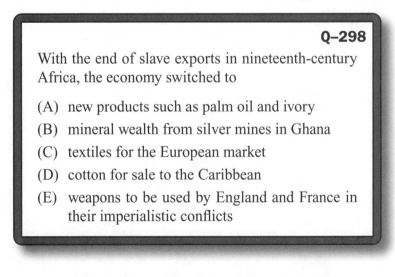

Q–298

With the end of slave exports in nineteenth-century Africa, the economy switched to

(A) new products such as palm oil and ivory

(B) mineral wealth from silver mines in Ghana

(C) textiles for the European market

(D) cotton for sale to the Caribbean

(E) weapons to be used by England and France in their imperialistic conflicts

Your Answer _____

_____

Correct Answers

A–297

(D) Russia attempted some reforms in the nineteenth century, but it still lagged behind the West in giving rights to its people. The Romanov tsars tended to be conservative and heavy-handed in dealing with dissent. All reforms were top-down, and the large peasant class lived in poverty. There was almost no merchant middle class to give stability to the nation.

A–298

(A) The African slave trade died slowly in the 1800s, mostly due to British pressure and laws in the United States banning the traffic in humans from overseas. Demand for other goods such as ivory and palm oil grew sharply, and plantations soon were growing coffee to sell to Europe. Textiles and weapons were made in Europe and then sold to other parts of the world; Africa lacked an industrial capability at this time.

 Take Test-Readiness Quiz 3 on CD
(to review questions 199–298)

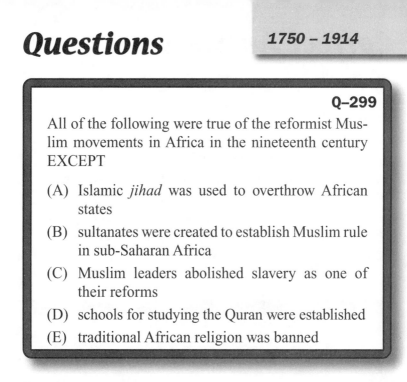

Q–299

All of the following were true of the reformist Muslim movements in Africa in the nineteenth century EXCEPT

(A) Islamic *jihad* was used to overthrow African states

(B) sultanates were created to establish Muslim rule in sub-Saharan Africa

(C) Muslim leaders abolished slavery as one of their reforms

(D) schools for studying the Quran were established

(E) traditional African religion was banned

Your Answer _____

_____

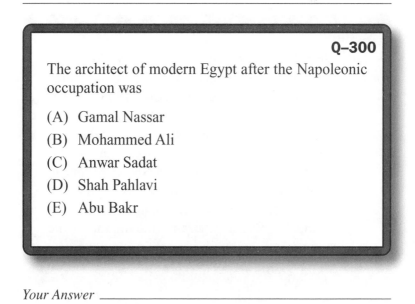

Q–300

The architect of modern Egypt after the Napoleonic occupation was

(A) Gamal Nassar

(B) Mohammed Ali

(C) Anwar Sadat

(D) Shah Pahlavi

(E) Abu Bakr

Your Answer _____

_____

Correct Answers

A–299

(C) Various Islamic reform movements took place in different parts of Africa after 1800. The tradition of *jihad* allowed for some military force to be applied in the name of God. This consolidated some sultanates and led to the spread of Islam beyond the Sahara region. Slavery remained part of the African economy, and a thriving trans-Saharan slave trade existed between West Africa and the Middle East.

A–300

(B) After the French had held Egypt briefly in the early 1800s, Egyptians saw how far behind they were compared to Europe. After 1805, Ali began to use Western methods to modernize his country, even as the British began to take control of some parts of the region. Islamic traditions were combined with some European approaches, which was a productive synthesis. Trade expanded, and the Egyptian economy was the most robust in Africa by the middle of the century.

Q–301

European military expeditions during the so-called Scramble for Africa were marked by

(A) mixed success because natives fought back in numerous parts of the continent

(B) complete domination over the continent within 10 years

(C) German stealing of colonies from the Dutch

(D) unsuccessful searches for precious metals

(E) few Protestant missions being established

Your Answer _____

_____

Q–302

The British rule of India could be characterized as

(A) complete political control of the subcontinent

(B) exercising limited impact in Bengal

(C) a steppingstone to control of Afghanistan

(D) free of rebellions by the natives.

(E) direct and indirect control over various parts of the subcontinent

Your Answer _____

_____

Correct Answers

A–301

(A) European military ventures in Africa during the late nineteenth century were ad hoc and sometimes unsuccessful. Natives were sometimes victorious and other times led resistance movements for decades against the Europeans. While many parts of the continent were eventually colonized by the Europeans, there were continuing frustrations with native resistance.

A–302

(E) British rule of India was a complex tapestry of direct rule and some alliances with Indian princes. Britain connected the region with its railroads and established its educational system in many parts of South Asia. Different arrangements were made with Indian rulers that created indirect protectorates over many subregions. The crown appointed a single British overseer called the viceroy who managed the vast British holdings.

Questions

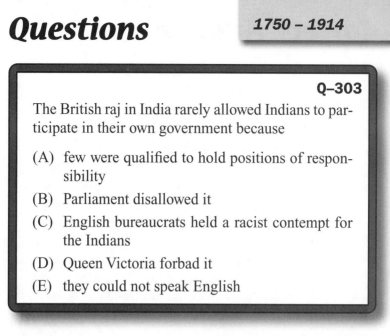

Q–303

The British raj in India rarely allowed Indians to participate in their own government because

(A) few were qualified to hold positions of responsibility

(B) Parliament disallowed it

(C) English bureaucrats held a racist contempt for the Indians

(D) Queen Victoria forbad it

(E) they could not speak English

Your Answer _____

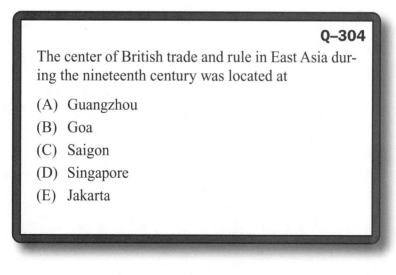

Q–304

The center of British trade and rule in East Asia during the nineteenth century was located at

(A) Guangzhou

(B) Goa

(C) Saigon

(D) Singapore

(E) Jakarta

Your Answer _____

Correct Answers

A–303

(C) British racism toward the Indians was common and widespread within the Indian Civil Service (ICS). The ICS was dominated by whites, and few Indians could pass the examinations. Equality with the natives was difficult for the majority of English people to grasp. So the natives remained a lesser society even as many of them became educated by the British. The educated Indians who were the products of this schooling would become the nationalists who would eventually resist British dominance.

A–304

(D) The British made impressive imperial gains in East Asia when they took territories in Malaya and Australia. For trading with China, they needed a major port at an Asian crossroads. Singapore is a small island at the tip of the Malay Peninsula and has a very good harbor. British and Chinese merchants soon made it a premier center of world trade.

Questions

Q–305

Which of the following developments made foreign goods cheaper throughout the nineteenth century?

(A) A period of relative peace in the world

(B) New faster ships that made voyages in half the time

(C) Lower taxes passed by governments

(D) The discovery of less expensive fuels

(E) The partitioning of Africa by Europe

Your Answer _____

Q–306

Some British colonies such as Georgia and Australia (New South Wales) started out as

(A) popular investments for wealthy capitalists

(B) refuges from the political strife of Europe

(C) places for the sick and infirm to immigrate to

(D) a dumping ground for convicts

(E) places for the religiously persecuted

Your Answer _____

317

Correct Answers

A–305

(B) Ships were transformed in the nineteenth century because faster clipper ships were both larger and more efficient to sail. Eventually steam-powered ships were able to cross oceans in little more than a week. The voyage from India to Britain used to take six months but by 1870, it could be done in three months. This brought down costs for importers and allowed them to lower their prices.

A–306

(D) Prisons in England were overflowing in the 1700s, and one solution was to offer low-risk convicts such as debtors a chance to leave the country. Convicts were both men and women who all chose a distant exile in return for their freedom. These colonies grew slowly and later, other immigrants populated these more remote colonies.

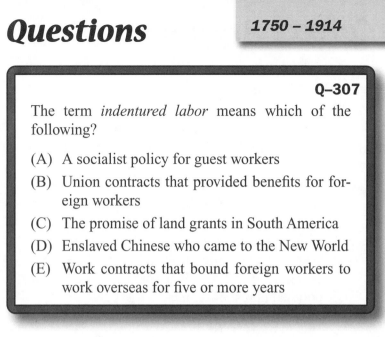

Q–307

The term *indentured labor* means which of the following?

(A) A socialist policy for guest workers

(B) Union contracts that provided benefits for foreign workers

(C) The promise of land grants in South America

(D) Enslaved Chinese who came to the New World

(E) Work contracts that bound foreign workers to work overseas for five or more years

Your Answer _____

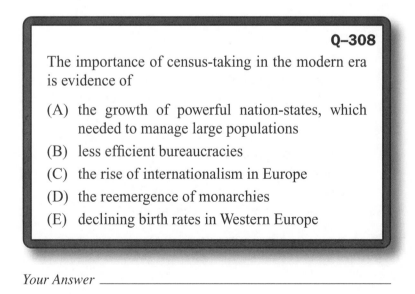

Q–308

The importance of census-taking in the modern era is evidence of

(A) the growth of powerful nation-states, which needed to manage large populations

(B) less efficient bureaucracies

(C) the rise of internationalism in Europe

(D) the reemergence of monarchies

(E) declining birth rates in Western Europe

Your Answer _____

Correct Answers

A–307

(E) Indentured workers, or "bond boys," were often young men who gave five to seven years of their lives to immigrate cost-free. They signed contracts in which they promised to work on plantations or farms for a certain number of years. After the contract was fulfilled, they could move where they wished. These workers were often poor rural workers in Europe or Asia who traded years for a new life far from home. Many were encouraged to leave their countries in times of political unrest or famine.

A–308

(A) As nations grew in size and power, they needed more information about themselves. One crucial statistic was the number of citizens in each country. Census-taking was important in determining political power, predicting economic trends, and managing the tax system. More money was spent on these periodic counts, and modern governments developed larger bureaucracies to handle the mechanism.

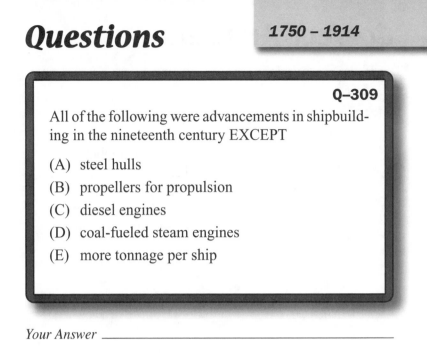

Q–309

All of the following were advancements in shipbuilding in the nineteenth century EXCEPT

(A) steel hulls

(B) propellers for propulsion

(C) diesel engines

(D) coal-fueled steam engines

(E) more tonnage per ship

Your Answer _____

_____

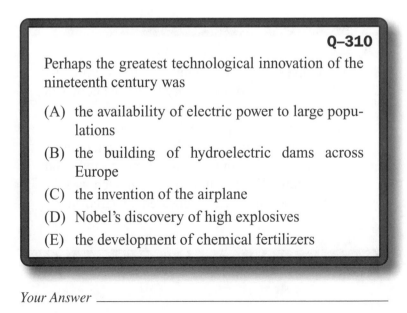

Q–310

Perhaps the greatest technological innovation of the nineteenth century was

(A) the availability of electric power to large populations

(B) the building of hydroelectric dams across Europe

(C) the invention of the airplane

(D) Nobel's discovery of high explosives

(E) the development of chemical fertilizers

Your Answer _____

_____

Correct Answers

A–309

(C) Ships became stronger, heavier, and faster in the 1800s. First, wood was replaced with iron and then steel as the main material for shipbuilding. Paddle wheels were exchanged for propellers, which were more efficient and speedier. The change from wind power to steam power made ships more maneuverable and able to sail in any direction.

A–310

(A) The lives of many people were transformed by the generation of electricity to private homes in the nineteenth century. At first, it was too expensive for most people, but new breakthroughs in power generation and the conduction of electricity allowed homes to be lit more safely and efficiently. Electric transportation such as subways and street cars appeared in large urban areas.

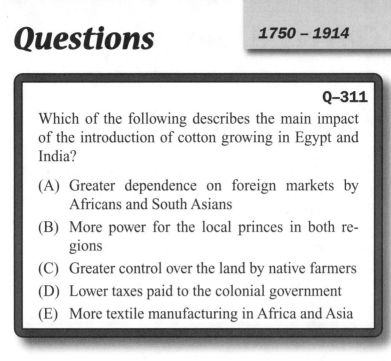

Q–311

Which of the following describes the main impact of the introduction of cotton growing in Egypt and India?

(A) Greater dependence on foreign markets by Africans and South Asians

(B) More power for the local princes in both regions

(C) Greater control over the land by native farmers

(D) Lower taxes paid to the colonial government

(E) More textile manufacturing in Africa and Asia

Your Answer _____

_____

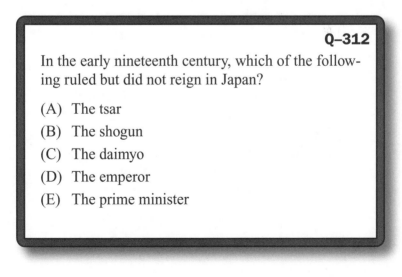

Q–312

In the early nineteenth century, which of the following ruled but did not reign in Japan?

(A) The tsar

(B) The shogun

(C) The daimyo

(D) The emperor

(E) The prime minister

Your Answer _____

_____

Correct Answers

A–311

(A) Increasing demand for raw material for textile manufacturing led to more cotton planting in overseas areas. Britain controlled large sections of India directly and had considerable influence over Egypt. Cheap cotton was shipped back to England and made into cloth. This could be re-exported back to the colonial areas, where it undersold local textiles. The end result was a close economic connection with colonial trade that was disadvantageous for India and countries like Egypt.

A–312

(B) Feudal Japan after 1600 was controlled by the Tokugawa shogun in Edo (present-day Tokyo). The shogun ruled over many feudal domains but allowed the emperor to live and reign in Kyoto. The emperor was a silent sovereign who had no political influence. In this way, Japan retained its imperial line but did not allow the emperor to venture out of west Japan.

Q–313

During the nineteenth century, the most desired Western technology in Asia was

(A) military weaponry

(B) medical hardware

(C) navigational know-how

(D) agricultural machinery

(E) animal husbandry

Your Answer _____

Q–314

The most important duty of middle-class European and American women in the nineteenth century was to

(A) take jobs to support their families

(B) obey their mothers-in-law

(C) prepare their sons and daughters for higher education

(D) raise their children at home

(E) enter the professional ranks after having children

Your Answer _____

Correct Answers

A–313

(A) In the nineteenth century, certain Asian nations wanted to learn all they could about modern military science and weaponry. Some, like China, made modest advances but still lost to Western navies and armies in wars. Others, like Japan, built up impressive military forces and even defeated European nations in war. The arms trade from Europe became a large export business as nations sought to develop modern military capabilities.

A–314

(D) During the Victorian era, middle-class women raised their own children and were stay-at-home mothers. They passed on housekeeping skills, such as embroidery and cooking, to their daughters. Most professional careers were difficult for women to enter. Some managed to go to medical school, but these women were extraordinary pioneers in their fields.

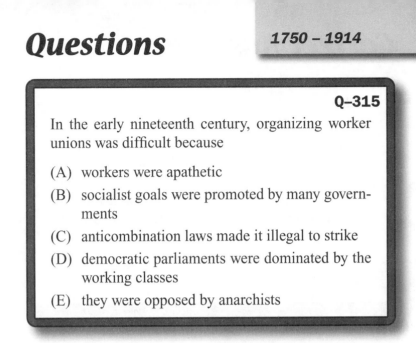

Q–315

In the early nineteenth century, organizing worker unions was difficult because

(A) workers were apathetic

(B) socialist goals were promoted by many governments

(C) anticombination laws made it illegal to strike

(D) democratic parliaments were dominated by the working classes

(E) they were opposed by anarchists

Your Answer _____

_____

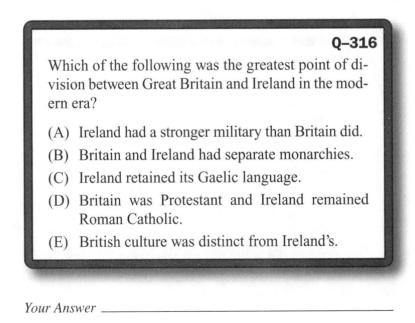

Q–316

Which of the following was the greatest point of division between Great Britain and Ireland in the modern era?

(A) Ireland had a stronger military than Britain did.

(B) Britain and Ireland had separate monarchies.

(C) Ireland retained its Gaelic language.

(D) Britain was Protestant and Ireland remained Roman Catholic.

(E) British culture was distinct from Ireland's.

Your Answer _____

_____

Correct Answers

A–315

(C) Prior to 1848, governments were unfriendly to labor reforms. Most union activities such as worker strikes were banned by laws in Germany, Britain, France, and other industrial nations. Only after 1850 were new laws passed that allowed workers to organize. By the end of the century, millions of workers were members of unions in Europe and the United States.

A–316

(D) Britain and Ireland have had contentious relations going back to medieval times. In the modern era, British control of Ireland created many conflicts and eventually led to partial independence for the Irish. Religious issues have remained central to their difficult relationship over time. The British sponsored Protestant immigration to Ireland to balance the cultural divide, but most Irish remained staunchly Catholic and saw the British as invaders.

Q–317

It is not the strongest of the species that survives, nor the most intelligent that survives. It is the one that is the most adaptable to change.

—Charles Darwin

This passage from *The Origin of the Species* refers to the concept of

(A) devolution

(B) natural selection

(C) animal socialization

(D) imperialism

(E) nationalism

Your Answer _____

Q–318

Which of the following had the greatest manufacturing capability from 1800 to 1914?

(A) China

(B) Canada

(C) France

(D) Great Britain

(E) Italy

Your Answer _____

Correct Answers

A–317

(B) Darwin was a naturalist who argued that the planet was much older than many people thought. He suggested that all species, from birds to humans, change over time depending on the environment they have to survive in. The idea of natural selection was radical in the late nineteenth century and created much discussion and controversy. Some used his theories to explain why some nations or races were superior to others, but Darwin was only investigating the zoological world.

A–318

(D) The first nation to industrialize was Great Britain. Through the nineteenth century, hundreds of British factories were built and produced goods that were sold all over the world. Other nations such as France and Italy did have some manufacturing ability in this time period but they could not compete with the British. Only the Americans and Germans could begin to rival the British by 1910.

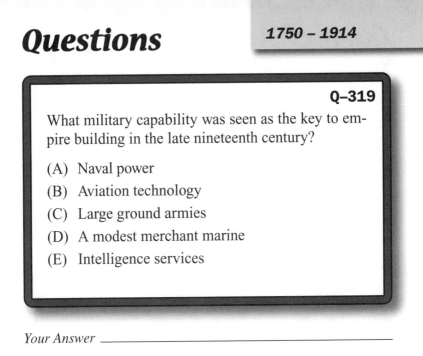

Q–319

What military capability was seen as the key to empire building in the late nineteenth century?

(A) Naval power

(B) Aviation technology

(C) Large ground armies

(D) A modest merchant marine

(E) Intelligence services

Your Answer _____

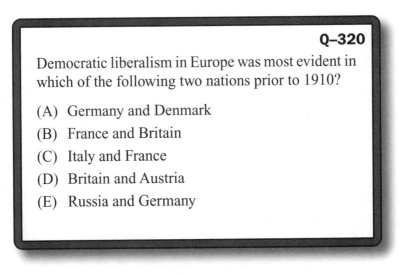

Q–320

Democratic liberalism in Europe was most evident in which of the following two nations prior to 1910?

(A) Germany and Denmark

(B) France and Britain

(C) Italy and France

(D) Britain and Austria

(E) Russia and Germany

Your Answer _____

Correct Answers

A–319

(A) Great Britain became the world model for empire building after 1815. It created the greatest empire in human history in part because it had a well-organized and powerful navy. Other industrial nations such as Germany, France, and the United States also built navies that could patrol the oceans and protect their interests at home and abroad. Bigger and faster battleships became the pride of leading powers prior to 1914.

A–320

(B) Liberal reforms that gave more political power to average people took root in France and Britain after the Age of Revolutions. Suffrage and labor reform made the most progress in Britain and France, while other nations clung to conservative monarchies that opposed liberal changes. Russia was the least progressive; Germany and Italy made modest progress prior to 1910.

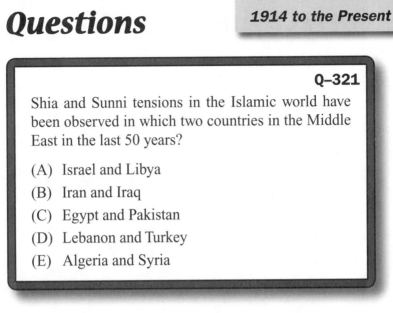

Q–321

Shia and Sunni tensions in the Islamic world have been observed in which two countries in the Middle East in the last 50 years?

(A) Israel and Libya

(B) Iran and Iraq

(C) Egypt and Pakistan

(D) Lebanon and Turkey

(E) Algeria and Syria

Your Answer _____

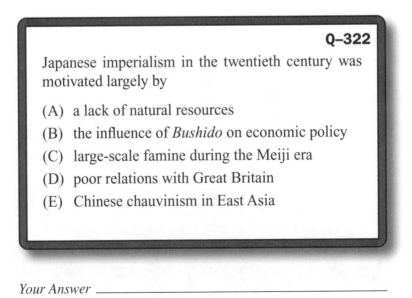

Q–322

Japanese imperialism in the twentieth century was motivated largely by

(A) a lack of natural resources

(B) the influence of *Bushido* on economic policy

(C) large-scale famine during the Meiji era

(D) poor relations with Great Britain

(E) Chinese chauvinism in East Asia

Your Answer _____

Correct Answers

A–321

(B) The area in the Middle East that has seen the most tension between Muslims in recent years is where Iraq and Iran are located. Formerly called Persia, Iran is where the most Shia live. Iraq also has many believers in the Shiite sect within its country. Tensions between the two branches of Islam have been evident within Iraq and also when the two nations went to war in the 1980s.

A–322

(A) Japan modernized very rapidly after 1870 and built an impressive military. The Japanese army and navy won significant campaigns against the Chinese and Russians by 1910. Its greatest challenge in developing an industrial base was its lack of resources. Importing raw materials from other nations put Japan at a distinct disadvantage. The Japanese government was dominated by conservative militarists, and they expanded to nearby Korea and China to gain the resources they lacked.

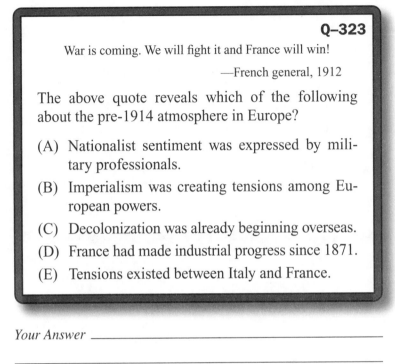

Q–323

War is coming. We will fight it and France will win!

—French general, 1912

The above quote reveals which of the following about the pre-1914 atmosphere in Europe?

(A) Nationalist sentiment was expressed by military professionals.

(B) Imperialism was creating tensions among European powers.

(C) Decolonization was already beginning overseas.

(D) France had made industrial progress since 1871.

(E) Tensions existed between Italy and France.

Your Answer _____

_____

Correct Answers

A–323

(A) Tensions between France and Germany had simmered since the Franco-Prussian War of 1871. French losses created a desire to avenge the nation. Nationalism was pronounced within the general staffs of many European nations. They planned for the next war and believed they would triumph quickly. Most nations believed the war would be quick and decisive.

Q–324

Which of the following describes the geopolitical situation in Europe prior to 1914?

(A) Great Britain was in decline, which inspired aggression in Central Europe.

(B) Russia and France were on the brink of war over the Balkans.

(C) War in Asia was draining the resources of some European powers.

(D) The rise of Germany and the decline of Ottoman Turkey were changing the power relationships within Europe.

(E) Revolts in Africa were causing the collapse of European imperialism.

Your Answer _____

_____

Correct Answers

A–324

(D) After 1860, Ottoman Turkey was referred to as the sick man of Europe. This meant that a once-mighty empire was in decline and causing a power vacuum in one part of the continent. At the same time, Germany had become the most powerful continental power, with a large, modern standing army. These two factors created specific regional tensions that would help bring war in 1914.

Q–325

Which of the following was the *immediate* cause of the Great War of 1914–1918?

(A) A political assassination in the Balkans

(B) Local tensions in Russia escalating into war

(C) A treaty between Russia and France that angered Germany

(D) A confrontation between France and Italy in Africa, which led to fighting

(E) Germany's invasion of Belgium in an attempt to increase its territory

Your Answer _____

Q–326

Which of the following was NOT a long-term cause of World War I?

(A) Imperialistic competition for foreign territories

(B) Defensive alliances among European powers

(C) Military build-up of navies and armies

(D) Socialist influences on governments

(E) Preplanned war movements

Your Answer _____

Correct Answers

A–325

(A) The Great War, or World War I, was started by an assassination in Sarajevo in 1914. The heir to the Austria-Hungarian throne was shot by a Serbian nationalist who wanted to incite his people to revolt against the Austrians. This led to an Austrian declaration of war against Serbia, which in turn led to other nations joining to help their allies.

A–326

(D) While socialism was making inroads in some nations, it did not create the atmosphere before 1914 that led to war. Powerful nations such as France, Britain, Germany, and Italy were building up their militaries in anticipation of a conflict. Generals created multiple war plans to be put into action should war come. Alliances were created that bound certain nations to one another should one of them be attacked. The summer of 1914 saw all these pieces play a role in turning a regional conflict in the Balkans into a global war.

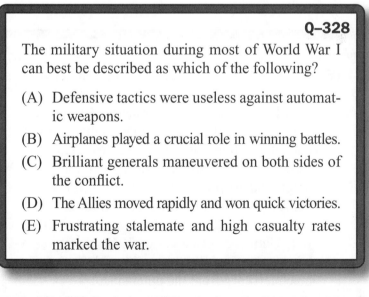

Q–327

Which of the following is true of both Germany and the United States by 1914?

(A) Both were monocultural nations.

(B) Both had low literacy rates among women.

(C) Labor unions had acquired great political power in both governments.

(D) Both had surpassed Great Britain in steel production.

(E) Both had large standing armies in case of war.

Your Answer _____

_____

Q–328

The military situation during most of World War I can best be described as which of the following?

(A) Defensive tactics were useless against automatic weapons.

(B) Airplanes played a crucial role in winning battles.

(C) Brilliant generals maneuvered on both sides of the conflict.

(D) The Allies moved rapidly and won quick victories.

(E) Frustrating stalemate and high casualty rates marked the war.

Your Answer _____

_____

Correct Answers

A–327

(D) Germany and the United States were the most dynamic industrial powers prior to World War I. They had grown rapidly during the nineteenth century, and their industries were the envy of the world. Large populations were available for factory work, and both had efficient managerial approaches to manufacturing. While Germany had the largest and most efficient army in the world, the United States had a modest military reserve system to use in case of war.

A–328

(E) World War I was a new kind of conflict with weapons such as the machine gun causing extraordinary death rates. Massive frontal assaults into rapid firing guns led to many deaths but little military advantage gained. Defensive works were built so that soldiers could live underground to protect them from artillery and bombings. The airplane was introduced as a weapon but had little impact on so vast a land war. Until the breakouts of 1918, there was a basic stalemate in which neither side could gain much territory from the other side.

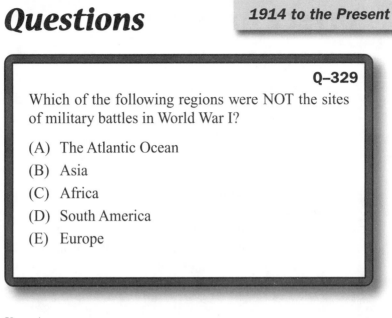

Q–329

Which of the following regions were NOT the sites of military battles in World War I?

(A) The Atlantic Ocean

(B) Asia

(C) Africa

(D) South America

(E) Europe

Your Answer _____

_____

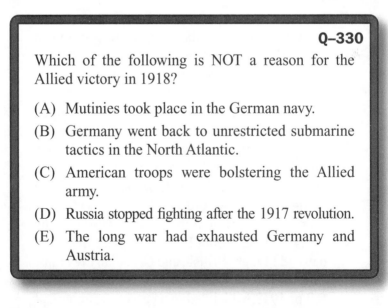

Q–330

Which of the following is NOT a reason for the Allied victory in 1918?

(A) Mutinies took place in the German navy.

(B) Germany went back to unrestricted submarine tactics in the North Atlantic.

(C) American troops were bolstering the Allied army.

(D) Russia stopped fighting after the 1917 revolution.

(E) The long war had exhausted Germany and Austria.

Your Answer _____

_____

Correct Answers

A–329

(D) World War I was the largest war to take place in so many different parts of the globe. While the main battles took place in Western and Eastern Europe, there were also colonial battles taking place in the Middle East, Africa, and the Far East. Navies fought on the high seas, and the new submarine technology meant that ships were vulnerable around the world. The North Atlantic was the scene of many attacks by German submarines on ships headed for France and Britain.

A–330

(D) The war in Europe had many unintended consequences, such as the Russian Revolution in 1917. The Bolsheviks took power in Russia and had promised to end the war. This was an advantage for the Germans because they could now concentrate their armies in the West and hoped for a breakthrough in the stalemate of that campaign. But after four years of numerous losses, morale was very low in many units on both sides. Some French and German units refused to fight or follow orders. When the Germans prompted the entry of the United States into the war, American troops began to replace many exhausted French, British, and Canadian divisions. This allowed for an Allied breakthrough in the fall of 1918, which led to a ceasefire agreement in November.

Q–331

Which of the following was NOT a result of the Great War from 1914 to 1918?

(A) Refugees were dislocated after losing their homes.

(B) Colonial power was enhanced overseas.

(C) Monarchies were toppled.

(D) Marxist movements gained strength in Europe.

(E) Nations lost territories when political boundaries were redrawn.

Your Answer _____

Correct Answers

A–331

(B) World War I had multiple effects around the world. It led to the collapse of three monarchies—in Austria, Germany, and Russia. Colonial power was weakened in Africa and Asia because France and England were unable to return to their former influence. The war destabilized governments, and radical movements on the right and the left gained more followers. The postwar settlement also changed the political boundaries in Europe and the Middle East, which led to other tensions after the end of the war.

Q–332

XIV. A general association of nations must be formed under specific covenants for the purpose of affording mutual guarantees of political independence and territorial integrity to great and small states alike.

—Woodrow Wilson, The Fourteen Points, 1918

The above excerpt refers to what international body established in the post–World War I era?

(A) The Organization of American States

(B) The League of Nations

(C) The European Union

(D) The United Nations

(E) The North Atlantic Treaty Organization

Your Answer _____

Correct Answers

A–332

(B) In 1918, the president of the United States laid out his Fourteen Points, which were a plan for peace after the Great War. His last point suggested a new international association of nations that would help keep the peace. This was debated at the treaty negotiations at Versailles after the war, when it was decided that the League of Nations be established. It was founded in 1920, with its headquarters in Switzerland.

Q–333

His Majesty's Government views with favour of the establishment in Palestine of a national home for the Jewish people, and will use their best endeavours to facilitate the achievement of this object, it being clearly understood that nothing shall be done which may prejudice the civil and religious rights of existing non-Jewish communities in Palestine, or the rights and political status enjoyed by Jews in any other country.

—Lord Balfour, Letter, 1917

The above quote fulfills the desires of which of the following twentieth-century movements?

(A) Pan-Slavism in the Balkans

(B) Zionism in Europe

(C) Pan-Arabism in the Middle East

(D) National Socialism in Germany

(E) Syrian nationalism in Asia Minor

Your Answer _____

_____

Correct Answers

A–333

(B) The letter, written in 1917, expressed some support by the British government for the Zionist movement that developed in the late nineteenth century in Europe. Nationalism took root in certain Jewish circles, which sought a homeland for Jewish people. Ottoman Turkey dominated the former geography of ancient Israel but tolerated some Jewish settlement after 1880. Influential Jewish leaders sought support for the idea of a Jewish state from important nations such as Britain.

Q–334

All of the following are features of twentieth-century fascism EXCEPT

(A) following pro-Marxist policies

(B) support of conservative business interests

(C) single-party rule

(D) ultranationalist themes used to inspire patriotism

(E) the build-up and promotion of militaries

Your Answer _____

_____

Q–335

In which region of the world do the largest number of Buddhists live?

(A) East Asia

(B) South America

(C) Central Asia

(D) Eastern Europe

(E) The Middle East

Your Answer _____

_____

Correct Answers

A–334

(A) Fascism arose as a reaction to Marxist revolution after World War I. Fascist movements were successful in gaining power in Europe and Latin America after 1920. Capitalist interests might support fascist leaders as long as communism and unionism were thwarted. Nationalism and militarism are central features of this ideology so that people would be prepared to fight for their country. Flags are used extensively to stimulate patriotism in the population and gather support for the government.

A–335

(A) Buddhism began in South Asia but did not thrive in the Hindu cultural environment. It was spread by missionaries to China and Southeast Asia, and found many converts over the centuries. In time, it also spread to Japan. Today more Buddhist temples are found in countries from Korea to Vietnam. Different sects of the religion have developed in different parts of Asia.

Questions

Q–336

All of the following helped cause the Russian Revolution of 1917 EXCEPT

(A) a long war had exhausted the military

(B) the death of the tsar weakened the government

(C) Germans helped Lenin return to Russia

(D) charismatic leadership spurred the radical revolutionaries

(E) widespread famine destabilized the nation

Your Answer _____

Q–337

Which of the following is true about the Treaty of Versailles in 1919?

(A) Land was reapportioned in Eastern Europe to create new countries.

(B) Germany was allowed to keep its army.

(C) Switzerland was enlarged at the expense of Austria.

(D) The kaiser gave up this throne to the crown prince.

(E) France gladly returned the Rhineland to Germany.

Your Answer _____

Correct Answers

A–336

(B) World War I brought about the downfall of the tsarist regime in Russia. Defeats on the battlefield left the army in shambles, and famine was common across the nation. The tsar abdicated and turned the government over to moderate socialists, who took charge briefly. The radical Bolsheviks then took over and placed the tsar under house arrest. Eventually they shot the entire royal family to end the monarchy.

A–337

(A) The Treaty of Versailles attempted to reorder Europe and keep the peace. Wilson had promised that people would be able to determine their own political future. Poland was repositioned on the map in Eastern Europe, and new nations such as Czechoslovakia were created out of the old Austrian empire. Germany lost its large army and its monarchy was abolished. France occupied portions of western Germany to extract mineral wealth from the defeated nation.

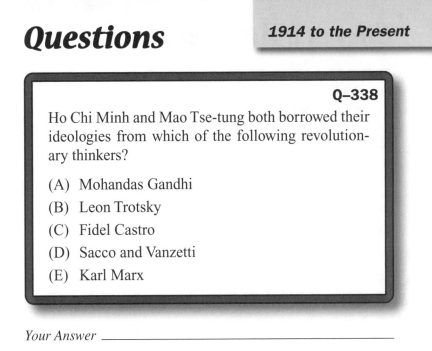

Q–338

Ho Chi Minh and Mao Tse-tung both borrowed their ideologies from which of the following revolutionary thinkers?

(A) Mohandas Gandhi

(B) Leon Trotsky

(C) Fidel Castro

(D) Sacco and Vanzetti

(E) Karl Marx

Your Answer _____

_____

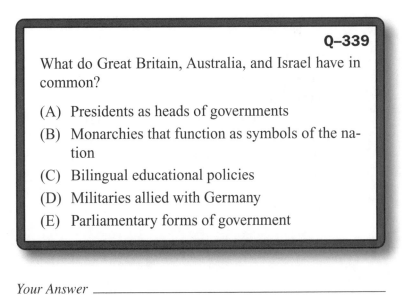

Q–339

What do Great Britain, Australia, and Israel have in common?

(A) Presidents as heads of governments

(B) Monarchies that function as symbols of the nation

(C) Bilingual educational policies

(D) Militaries allied with Germany

(E) Parliamentary forms of government

Your Answer _____

_____

Correct Answers

A–338

(E) Ho Chi Minh and Mao Tse-tung were both twentieth-century Marxist revolutionaries in East Asia. Ho became the father of modern Vietnam, while Mao founded the People's Republic of China in 1949. Both borrowed heavily from Marxist ideas about the workers needing to overthrow imperialist capitalism.

A–339

(E) Great Britain, Australia, and Israel all have prime ministers as the heads of their governments. They have parliaments that are elected by the people and form the national governments. They all have monolingual language policies. All are industrial nations with high-tech infrastructures.

Q–340

Which of the following countries grew to have the largest population in the world in the twentieth century?

(A) China

(B) Russia

(C) India

(D) Canada

(E) Indonesia

Your Answer _____

_____

Q–341

All of the following were accomplished by Kemal in establishing modern Turkey EXCEPT

(A) Muslim courts were suppressed

(B) women were not allowed to wear veils

(C) European laws were introduced

(D) the Arabic alphabet was retained

(E) Turkey was declared a secular republic

Your Answer _____

_____

Correct Answers

A–340

(A) By 1900, China had over 400 million people. This growth continued until the population topped 1 billion in the 1960s. Most Chinese were poor peasants who barely survived as farmers. Revolution and war characterized the twentieth-century Chinese experience, and tens of millions of people were killed across the country.

A–341

(D) Mustafa Kemal, also known as Atatürk, is the father of modern Turkey and radically remade the country after defeat in World War I. He was a military hero and father figure who wanted to make Turkey into a modern European nation. To do this, he reformed education and took power away from Muslim clerics. He did away with the Arabic alphabet and replaced it with a Romanized Latin writing system that is still in use today.

Q-342

Japan turned to a right-wing militaristic government in the 1920s and 1930s because of which of the following?

(A) Postwar nationalism and the Great Depression weakened democracy.

(B) A powerful shogun took control in Tokyo.

(C) The emperor became imperialistic after World War I.

(D) Liberal democracy led to labor riots.

(E) The Diet was dominated by socialists.

Your Answer _____

Q-343

The great twentieth-century physicist credited with the theory of relativity is

(A) James Newtron

(B) Niels Bohr

(C) Robert Oppenheimer

(D) Albert Einstein

(E) Max Planck

Your Answer _____

Correct Answers

A–342

(A) Japan was on the winning side of World War I but did not receive what it wanted in the peace settlement of 1919. Many nationalists protested and wanted Japan to assert itself on the world scene. Liberals were under siege as the military took more and more control of the government. The global depression further weakened the government, which was finally dominated by the army and navy.

A–343

(D) The older model of Newtonian physics was rethought when Einstein published his theory of relativity in the early twentieth century. He theorized that matter, space, and time were not fixed but relative to one another. New theories about the nature of light and the universe followed. This amounted to a revolution in terms of human understanding of the universe.

Questions

Q–344

After World War I, the former Ottoman empire was partitioned into new nations including

(A) Ethiopia and Oman

(B) Israel and Lebanon

(C) Jordan and Iraq

(D) Libya and Albania

(E) Egypt and Macedonia

Your Answer —————————————————————

Q–345

We want to glorify war, the world's only hygiene-militarism, pure in deed, destroyer of anarch-isms, ...

—Filippo Marinetti, 1920

The above slogan relates to which twentieth-century political phenomenon?

(A) Trade unionism

(B) Marxist revolutionary movements

(C) Italian fascism in the interwar period.

(D) Wilsonian democracy

(E) Liberal positivism

Your Answer —————————————————————

Correct Answers

A–344

(C) The Ottoman Turks had allied themselves with Germany and were defeated by the Western powers. The Ottoman empire lost its territories in the Middle East, and new nations were created. These new nations included Iran, Iraq, Jordan, Lebanon, Syria, and Saudi Arabia. As new nations, they were overseen by Britain and France for a time under League of Nations mandates.

A–345

(C) After the Treaty of Versailles, numerous nations —including Italy—were dissatisfied with the settlement. Some Italian nationalists dreamed of a strong nation led by military men who glorified war and masculine struggle. Benito Mussolini became the spokesperson for this new political ideology and took power in Italy after 1922. Fascists believed that war was the great endeavor of powerful nations, so they built up their armies to fight and expand their territories.

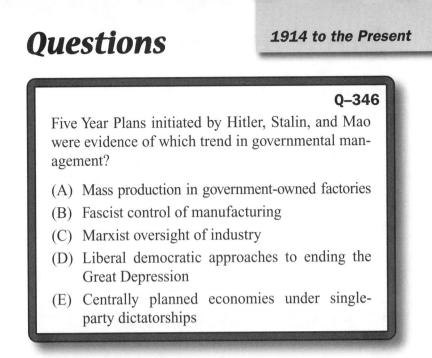

Q–346

Five Year Plans initiated by Hitler, Stalin, and Mao were evidence of which trend in governmental management?

(A) Mass production in government-owned factories

(B) Fascist control of manufacturing

(C) Marxist oversight of industry

(D) Liberal democratic approaches to ending the Great Depression

(E) Centrally planned economies under single-party dictatorships

Your Answer _____

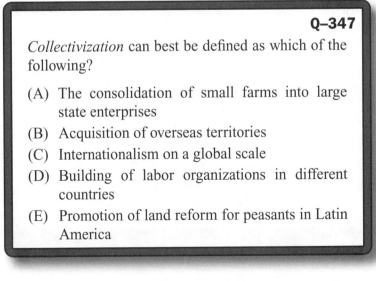

Q–347

Collectivization can best be defined as which of the following?

(A) The consolidation of small farms into large state enterprises

(B) Acquisition of overseas territories

(C) Internationalism on a global scale

(D) Building of labor organizations in different countries

(E) Promotion of land reform for peasants in Latin America

Your Answer _____

Correct Answers

A–346

(E) Powerful dictators took control of Germany, Russia, and China in the middle of the twentieth century. Some were fascist and others were Marxist, but they all sought to control their nations. While Germany allowed for private investment, the Soviet Union and China became communistic, with complete government control of the economy. Dictators on the right and left tried to plan their national economies so they would develop and grow stronger.

A–347

(A) After the revolution, Stalin began to create large-scale agricultural enterprises to control national farming and the people who worked the land. Many resisted and were starved or imprisoned by the Soviet dictator. Machinery and mass production were used to modernize Russian farming. Only obedient farmers survived the transition, and finally land was brought under government control by the 1930s.

Q–348

Economic depression is characterized by all of the following EXCEPT

(A) bank failures

(B) rampant inflation

(C) high unemployment

(D) collapse of the equity markets

(E) declining prices

Your Answer _____

_____

Q–349

All of the following destabilized international relations in the 1930s EXCEPT

(A) the Munich Agreement of 1938

(B) Japan's invasion of Manchuria

(C) Hitler's annexation of Austria

(D) Italy's invasion of Ethiopia

(E) Lenin's death in Russia

Your Answer _____

_____

Correct Answers

A–348

(B) Economic depression is defined as a long-term shrinking of the economy. Economic depressions have tended to occur periodically in history, and the most severe world depression took place in the 1930s. Depressions are characterized by the closing of both companies and banks. Panic results in large-scale selling in the stock markets and plummeting share prices. Prices for goods fall as demand decreases and money is scarce. Workers are laid off and joblessness increases dramatically. Inflation occurs with the rising of consumer prices and cannot occur during a depression.

A–349

(E) Strong and aggressive military regimes took power in Japan, Germany, and Italy in the 1930s. Each nation used its military forces to take territories and thus expand its power. Germany absorbed Austria and took Czechoslovakia with the Munich accord in 1938. Japan took northern China, and Italy invaded East Africa. All these acts of aggression weakened the liberal powers in the West and made war more likely. Lenin had died in 1924, which led to the rise of Stalin in the Soviet Union.

Questions

Q–350

The scene above is evidence of what twentieth-century political phenomenon?

(A) Children being drafted into the military

(B) Race riots in major cities

(C) Labor strikes in Harlem

(D) African-American patriotism

(E) Religious parades in New York

Your Answer _____

_____

Correct Answers

A–350

(D) The photograph shows the celebrations that took place as African-Americans returned home to their families after fighting in World War I. Nations drafted many young men to fight in their armies. African-Americans fought in the U.S. army in France and came home to victory parades and celebrations attended by their families. Men of all races fought around the world in different armies.

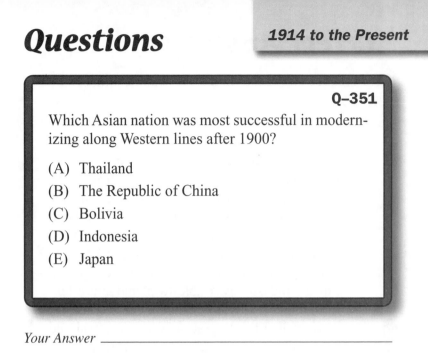

Q–351

Which Asian nation was most successful in modernizing along Western lines after 1900?

(A) Thailand

(B) The Republic of China

(C) Bolivia

(D) Indonesia

(E) Japan

Your Answer _____

_____

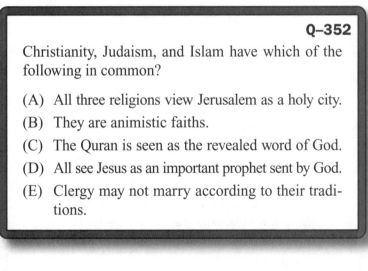

Q–352

Christianity, Judaism, and Islam have which of the following in common?

(A) All three religions view Jerusalem as a holy city.

(B) They are animistic faiths.

(C) The Quran is seen as the revealed word of God.

(D) All see Jesus as an important prophet sent by God.

(E) Clergy may not marry according to their traditions.

Your Answer _____

_____

Correct Answers

A–351

(E) The intrusion of the West influenced every Asian nation after 1700. Most resisted the Europeans but could not keep them out over the long term. Japan also tried to fend off the West but was pressured into opening trade with the Americans in the nineteenth century. The Japanese then became disciplined students of Western technology in many fields and succeeded in building a modern nation with a large military. Japan's industry was able to manufacture textiles, high-quality steel, and other goods. By 1940, it had the largest navy in the world and was ready to engage the West in a titanic war over control of the Pacific.

A–352

(A) All of the three monotheisms were born in the deserts of the Middle East. Judaism is the parent faith to the other two religions because Jesus was a Jew, and Mohammed saw himself as a continuation of Hebrew and Christian revelation from God. Jerusalem plays a role in all three religions. Stories take place there involving many personalities such as King David, Jesus, Saint Peter, Mohammed, and others. Followers of all three monotheisms have traveled to Jerusalem to worship and see the holy sites from the Bible and the Quran.

Questions

Q–353

All of the following were factors in the rise of Nazism in Germany EXCEPT

(A) the perception that the Treaty of Versailles was unjust

(B) Germans being drawn to Western liberalism

(C) fear of communism taking root

(D) political instability resulting from the Great Depression

(E) Hitler's appeals to German pride because he promised a stronger nation

Your Answer _____

_____

Q–354

Which of the following were twentieth-century fascist nations?

(A) Canada and Spain

(B) Germany and Russia

(C) Poland and Italy

(D) Nicaragua and Mexico

(E) Italy and Spain

Your Answer _____

_____

Correct Answers

A–353

(B) Germany was saddled with large war debts after the Great War ended. The economy suffered rampant inflation and then the devastation of the global depression in the 1930s. The success of communism in nearby Russia also caused anxiety in the middle and upper classes. Hitler crafted an appealing message of returning Germany to greatness. He promised to tear up the Treaty of Versailles and rebuild the military.

A–354

(E) Fascism took root in several nations in the twentieth century. Some of these countries were in Europe and others in Latin America. The most well-known fascist governments were established in Europe in the 1920s and 1930s. Italy was the first nation to adopt a right-wing fascist government, but both Germany and Spain followed with militaristic dictatorships of their own.

Q–355

Which of the following were great advantages for the Allies in their victory over the Axis nations in World War II?

(A) New technologies such as rockets

(B) Stronger navies at the start of the conflict

(C) Abundant natural resources and large populations

(D) Shorter supply lines

(E) Support from African nations

Your Answer _____

Q–356

All of the following were new technologies adapted to warfare in World War II EXCEPT

(A) armored tanks

(B) long-range missiles

(C) nuclear bombs

(D) jet aircraft

(E) radar

Your Answer _____

Correct Answers

A–355

(C) After the Soviet Union and the United States entered the war in 1941, the Axis nations faced two very large and resourceful nations. The United States was already the most productive industrial nation in the world and could manufacture large quantities of material for the war effort. The Soviet Union had a large population to contribute and was able to design weaponry to counter the German assault on its territory. The advantage of natural resources, which Japan and Germany lacked, was a decisive advantage in a long protracted war.

A–356

(A) World War II saw the introduction of many new technologies used to fight the war on both sides. The Germans made impressive advances in rocketry and launched the first long-range missiles that delivered explosives to foreign cities. They also produced the first jet aircraft used in war. The British developed radar to detect aircraft from a distance, and the Americans developed the atomic bomb to use on Japan in the last month of the war. Tanks had already been produced during World War I, a generation earlier.

Q–357

Appeasement is best defined as which of the following?

(A) Bilateral negotiations between enemy states

(B) The desire for peace, leading to concessions with another powerful nation

(C) Protests against aggression by an international body

(D) Appealing to the world community for aid

(E) Surrogate fighting in another country

Your Answer _____

Q–358

The concept of collective security is best represented in the twentieth century by the creation of

(A) the Comintern

(B) large militaries by some nations

(C) bilateral treaties

(D) the League of Nations

(E) the G8 organization

Your Answer _____

Correct Answers

A–357

(B) The term *appeasement* has often been used to describe the events of 1938 when Germany demanded territorial adjustments in Central Europe. Hitler believed that the Treaty of Versailles had not taken ethnic Germans into consideration, so he demanded control over the border region of Czechoslovakia. Britain and France negotiated a settlement that allowed Germany to take parts of Czechoslovakia in return for a promise that Hitler would keep the peace. That agreement has been criticized as a precursor to World War II because Hitler was not satisfied with the Czech settlement and later invaded Poland.

A–358

(D) After the horrors of modern war in World War I, nations tried to come up with a mechanism to prevent another conflict. The League of Nations was envisioned as an organization that would provide international pressure in case war were to break out somewhere in the world. If one country were to break the peace and start war, other nations would force an aggressor to back down. This concept of collective security meant that all nations would be more secure if they worked together to keep war from escalating into global conflict.

Q–359

The euphemism *Greater East Asian Co-prosperity Sphere* was used by Japan in World War II to refer to

(A) the commonwealth of former British colonies

(B) former French colonies in Asia

(C) Anglo-Japanese colonies in the Pacific

(D) territories conquered by their military and included in their empire

(E) free trade occurring in their region

Your Answer _____

Q–360

Japanese and German crimes against humanity during World War II included all of the following EXCEPT

(A) using prisoners of war in cruel medical experiments

(B) mass murder of selected ethnic groups

(C) forced prostitution of colonial women during the war

(D) torture of prisoners captured in battle

(E) unleashing chemical weapons in major battles

Your Answer _____

Correct Answers

A–359

(D) Japan tried to appeal to fellow Asians by suggesting that they create an anti-imperialistic zone under Japanese control. This meant expelling the Europeans from Asia and, while some Indians, Indonesians, and Malaysians did collaborate with the Japanese to fight the Europeans, many saw this appeal as a way to replace one imperialist with another. Propaganda from Tokyo continued to publicize the Japanese triumphs over the British and the Dutch, but many Asians fought Japan and helped the Allies during the war.

A–360

(E) Both Germany and Japan were held responsible for atrocities during World War II. These international trials or tribunals sought to set a precedent for prosecuting people who had behaved barbarously in time of war. Both the Germans and Japanese conducted medical experiments on Russians and Chinese in prisoner camps. Special military units also participated in the torture of people who opposed the military occupations of the Axis nations. Numerous German and Japanese military and government officials were tried and executed after the war by the Allied military courts.

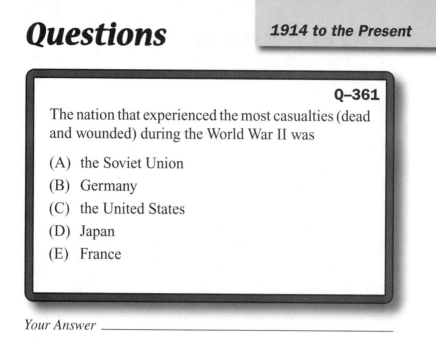

Q–361

The nation that experienced the most casualties (dead and wounded) during the World War II was

(A) the Soviet Union

(B) Germany

(C) the United States

(D) Japan

(E) France

Your Answer _____

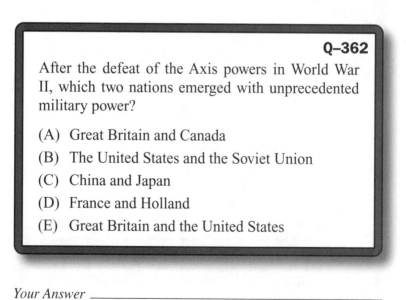

Q–362

After the defeat of the Axis powers in World War II, which two nations emerged with unprecedented military power?

(A) Great Britain and Canada

(B) The United States and the Soviet Union

(C) China and Japan

(D) France and Holland

(E) Great Britain and the United States

Your Answer _____

Correct Answers

A–361

(A) It is estimated that over 50 million people died in World War II. The war between Germany and Russia was particularly gruesome and hard-fought, and left as many as 20 million Russians dead. Both sides set aside the conventional rules of combat and fought one another without restraint. While many more Russians died in the battles fought, the Germans were eventually invaded by Russia and defeated in 1945.

A–362

(B) With the massive destruction of World War II, only two nations had the resources and populations to continue as true world powers. Japan and Germany were utterly defeated and had to reconstitute their governments and economies. Britain and France had exhausted their treasuries and were victorious but weak. China was deeply divided between the nationalist leadership and communist movements in the countryside. Only the United States and the Soviet Union had large standing armies and possessed abundant resources after 1945. The term *superpower* was coined to describe the United States and the Soviet Union in the postwar period.

Q–363

The term *cold war* best refers to which of the following in history?

(A) Colonial conflicts between different Marxist groups

(B) Peace negotiations between Middle Eastern nations

(C) Decolonization in Africa after 1945

(D) Naval tensions in the cold North Atlantic Ocean

(E) Two hostile camps, communist and capitalist, contending for influence

Your Answer _____

Q–364

Containment can best be defined as which of the following after 1945?

(A) Giving aid to war-torn nations in the name of peace

(B) Arms agreements between the United States and the Soviet Union

(C) New environmental programs to stop pollution

(D) The American policy to stop the spread of communism in the world

(E) Chinese communist propaganda against the West

Your Answer _____

Correct Answers

A–363

(E) World War II caused large shifts in world power. After the surrender of the Axis powers in Tokyo and Berlin, the Allies wielded great influence during the postwar order. A new rivalry arose between democratic/liberal states led by the United States and communist/revolutionary states led by the Soviet Union. For decades after 1945, the Cold War created numerous regional conflicts in which the Americans and Russians sought domination over the other.

A–364

(D) In 1947, American attitudes toward Soviet communism were evolving. A former World War II ally, the Soviet Union was now seen as a threat to democracy around the world. George Kennan, a top expert on the Soviet Union, wrote a paper suggesting that the United States seek to limit the influence of the Soviet Union. This policy would become an overarching goal to work around the world to "contain" communism where it existed.

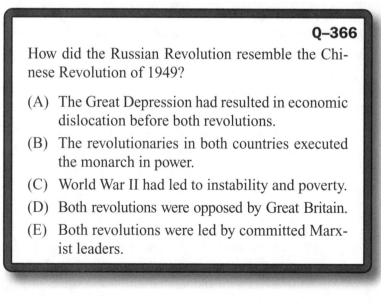

Q-365

The most influential factor in the weakening of European empires after 1945 was

(A) the liberalization of world trade

(B) the victory of world communism in Asia and Africa

(C) the industrialization of Asia and South America

(D) the rise of nationalism that was prompted by both world wars

(E) postwar prosperity in the Third World

Your Answer _____

_____

Q-366

How did the Russian Revolution resemble the Chinese Revolution of 1949?

(A) The Great Depression had resulted in economic dislocation before both revolutions.

(B) The revolutionaries in both countries executed the monarch in power.

(C) World War II had led to instability and poverty.

(D) Both revolutions were opposed by Great Britain.

(E) Both revolutions were led by committed Marxist leaders.

Your Answer _____

_____

Correct Answers

A–365

(D) The Age of Imperialism was at its peak prior to World War I as European nations competed for foreign territories in Asia and Africa. Both World War I and World War II dealt severe blows to European powers and also encouraged Asian and African nationalism. Even victorious powers such as Britain and France suffered greatly in fighting the long and costly wars of the twentieth century. After 1945, they tried unsuccessfully to retain their empires but no longer had the will or resources to do so. One by one, Asian and African nations fought for and won their independence. By 1970, little was left of European power in the Southern and Eastern hemispheres.

A–366

(E) The Russian Revolution of 1917 was the first Marxist overthrow of an existing government. The tsarist regime had been weakened greatly by World War I and it helped create opportunities for the radical Bolsheviks. A generation later, World War II also weakened the nationalists in China and helped the communists under Mao Tse-tung take control. Like Lenin in Russia in 1917, Mao used Marxist ideas to appeal to the poor and dispossessed in China. He preached the overthrow of the landed elites and the capitalist classes.

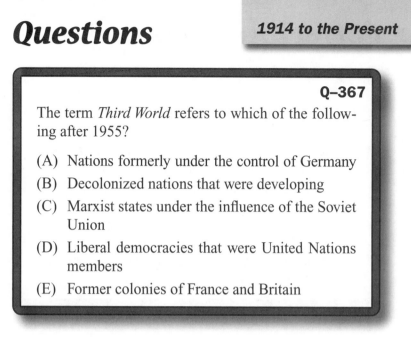

Q–367

The term *Third World* refers to which of the following after 1955?

(A) Nations formerly under the control of Germany

(B) Decolonized nations that were developing

(C) Marxist states under the influence of the Soviet Union

(D) Liberal democracies that were United Nations members

(E) Former colonies of France and Britain

Your Answer _____

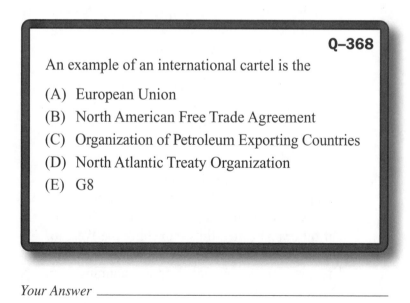

Q–368

An example of an international cartel is the

(A) European Union

(B) North American Free Trade Agreement

(C) Organization of Petroleum Exporting Countries

(D) North Atlantic Treaty Organization

(E) G8

Your Answer _____

Correct Answers

A–367

(B) In the early 1950s the term *Third World* began to be used to refer to nations that were less developed and did not fit into the capitalist or communist blocs. These nations were emerging from colonialism and tended to be in the Southern Hemisphere. The term also began to suggest a nonaligned position of being neither communist nor capitalist. By 1965, most of the nations in the world could be called Third World and they made up the majority of the United Nations membership.

A–368

(C) Companies are called multinationals when they conduct business in multiple nations. Nations sometimes combine into economic organizations for mutual benefit. In 1960, some nations possessing oil banded together to discuss common issues. They became known as the Organization of Petroleum Exporting Countries (OPEC) and would sometimes agree to decrease or increase production to influence oil prices worldwide. This cartel could then fix prices and control consumption. After the Yom Kippur War in 1973, some Islamic oil-producing nations used their power to raise the price of oil dramatically, thus punishing the West for its support of Israel during the war. Oil exports have become a political weapon stemming from Middle Eastern conflict.

Questions

Q–369

Which of the following would best characterize post–World War II Japan?

(A) An industrial export economy that ranked in the top five worldwide

(B) An advocate of free trade

(C) A nonaligned country that distanced itself from the superpowers

(D) A revived military power in East Asia

(E) Unable to compete with Korea in the world marketplace

Your Answer _____

Q–370

Gandhi's vision for an independent India can best be summed up as a

(A) socialist state that favored Hindus

(B) secular Marxist nation

(C) combination of Hindu and Buddhist values

(D) theocratic state dominated by Brahmins

(E) democratic, secular state

Your Answer _____

Correct Answers

A–369

(A) Japan was occupied by the U.S. army after World War II and was guided toward a democratic system. Economically, it began a gradual but finally spectacular recovery as its industry boomed and successfully sold goods all over the world. Still resource-poor, Japan returned to the top tier of industrialized nations within one generation of its defeat in 1945. By 1980, it ranked behind only Germany and the United States in terms of industrial output.

A–370

(E) Gandhi spent his life working for a free and independent India. His vision was for a secular state that protected the rights of all Indians regardless of their religious beliefs. A lawyer by training, he believed in the rule of law and the rights of the people. When Muslims wanted a separate nation, Gandhi fasted to show his disapproval, urging all Indians to join him in his belief in a free and tolerant India.

Q–371

Which of the following are examples of the work of the United Nations since 1945?

I.   Promoting cultural and educational programs worldwide

II. Helping newly independent nations establish themselves

III. Dealing with crises that lead to war

IV. Promoting human rights around the world

(A) I, II, and IV only

(B) I and II only

(C) III and IV only

(D) I, II, III, and IV

(E) I and IV only

Your Answer _____

_____

Correct Answers

A–371

(D) The United Nations (UN) was founded in 1945 as a peace keeping organization in the aftermath of the worst war in human history. The five Allied victors of the war—the United States, the Soviet Union, China, Great Britain, and France—were charter members. The United Nations has grown to over 190 nations as former colonies became new countries, and it has multiple bodies that deal with economic issues, security problems, and international law. It has promoted an international understanding of basic human rights around the world.

Q–372

Which regional crisis led to the first military intervention by the United Nations after 1945?

(A) The Greek Civil War

(B) The Israeli War of Independence

(C) The Chinese Civil War

(D) The Korean conflict

(E) The Vietnam War

Your Answer _____

Q–373

The women's movement in the early twentieth century was defined by the struggle to win

(A) workers' rights in the factories

(B) the right to vote

(C) access to birth control

(D) higher pay in the work place

(E) more seats in national legislatures

Your Answer _____

Correct Answers

A–372

(D) The United Nations created the Security Council to react to conflicts in the world. This small executive committee meets when tensions flare up somewhere in the world. The invasion of South Korea was one of the first tests of the United Nations' ability to maintain the peace and to react as a global body. The United Nations condemned the action and in the end sent troops to fight and protect the South Koreans. This was the first UN war in which collective security was put into practice. The resulting war lasted three years, until a ceasefire was negotiated to stop the fighting.

A–373

(B) The fight for female equality began in the nineteenth century as reforms such as workers' rights and abolition were advanced by women. Women in the industrial West campaigned and organized to achieve many different progressive goals into the twentieth century. The most crucial right fought for was the franchise, or right to vote. Suffragettes in Great Britain and the United States petitioned their governments for the right to vote but were often ignored. After decades of struggle, women finally were able to vote in some nations.

Q–374

Marxist revolutions took place after 1945 in which of the following nations?

(A) Nicaragua and Guatemala

(B) China and Cuba

(C) Canada and Angola

(D) Vietnam and India

(E) Greece and Albania

Your Answer _____

_____

Q–375

The rapid development of space technology was largely a byproduct of

(A) Sino-Soviet tensions

(B) new aviation breakthroughs in Japan

(C) science clubs in the United States

(D) European cooperation in forming a joint endeavor

(E) competition between the United States and the Soviet Union after World War II

Your Answer _____

_____

Correct Answers

A–374

(B) The gap between rich and poor inspired revolutions in various countries after 1945. The civil war in China led to a communist victory over the Nationalists in 1949 and the founding of the People's Republic of China. Later, in the 1950s, socialists in Cuba also overthrew the right-wing dictator and set up a Marxist state. Countries such as Vietnam, Albania, and Nicaragua also had Marxist governments at times.

A–375

(E) Germany was the first nation to make dramatic breakthroughs in missile technology in the twentieth century. After the war, the American and Soviet armies raced to capture top German scientists to find out what they knew. Both the superpowers spent great sums of money and time to build better and more powerful rockets that could go into outer space. The Soviets were the first to send a satellite and a human being into orbit around the earth. The Americans countered with their own satellites and also sent men into orbit. By the 1960s, a competition was under way to send rockets and even people to the moon. The United States put the first men on the moon in 1969 after spending billions of dollars to overtake the Soviet lead in space.

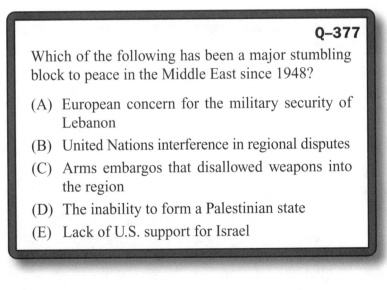

Q–376

Which of the following best explains the reason for the partition of India in 1947?

(A) Marxist rebels destabilized the political situation.

(B) Many Muslims and Hindus could not support Gandhi's multicultural vision.

(C) Sikh nationalists could not participate in a secular state.

(D) Jinnah lost popularity by supporting Gandhi.

(E) Nehru was assassinated by a Hindu extremist.

Your Answer _____

Q–377

Which of the following has been a major stumbling block to peace in the Middle East since 1948?

(A) European concern for the military security of Lebanon

(B) United Nations interference in regional disputes

(C) Arms embargos that disallowed weapons into the region

(D) The inability to form a Palestinian state

(E) Lack of U.S. support for Israel

Your Answer _____

Correct Answers

A–376

(B) The Congress Party had members of every religious group in India, but tensions eventually resulted in disagreement as independence drew closer. Muslim nationalists began to ask for their own nation, while Gandhi did everything he could to dissuade them from breaking away. Some Hindu extremists also did not support Gandhi's tolerant views and this resulted in Gandhi's assassination. The result was a partition of the former British colony, with Muslim territory on either side of the larger India.

A–377

(D) The establishment of Israel took place in the chaotic aftermath of World War II. While many people sympathized with the Zionist goals of Jews to have their own nation, the Arab people living in Palestine were bitter about losing their lands and communities when war broke out in the late 1940s. The dispossessed Palestinians became a political feature of the region, and this led to terrorism in the 1960s and 1970s. All the wars fought by Israelis and Arabs since 1948 have not resolved the central problem of the Palestinians, who continue to wish for a state of their own.

Q–378

The postwar success of decolonization in Africa and Asia has often depended on

(A) the amount of aid given to help newly forming nations

(B) the preparation of native elites for leadership by their colonial masters

(C) the influence of the Cold War on new states

(D) the sympathy of the West with regard to under-developed nations

(E) regional peace being possible

Your Answer _____

_____

Correct Answers

A–378

(B) Most successful transitions from colonial rule to independence have been overseen by well-educated native leaders such as Gandhi and Ho Chi Minh. These men were schooled by the British and French, which gave them a dual perspective of Western and non-Western viewpoints. Other colonial powers such as Portugal and Belgium did not prepare their former colonies as well for independence. All new nations in Africa and Asia faced many challenges after 1950. Some descended into civil war and great violence, while others wrote constitutions and embarked on a more defined political path.

Q–379

Which of the following would best describe the political character of Latin American states in the decades after World War II?

(A) Right-wing military regimes outnumbered democracies in the region.

(B) Communist states proliferated throughout South America.

(C) Democracy became the dominant political approach.

(D) Landless peasants overthrew oligarchies in most Central American states.

(E) The Cold War meant that most Latin American nations were nonaligned.

Your Answer _____

_____

Correct Answers

A–379

(A) Latin America saw modernization lead to the concentration of wealth in many nations after World War II. Landed elites retained both wealth and political power in many nations such as Argentina, Guatemala, and Chile. The trend was conservative leadership using the military to control the poorer population, which led to fascist states. In the 1970s, few nations, such as Colombia and Costa Rica, were democratic. Revolutions in both Cuba and Nicaragua led to dictators being overthrown by left-wing groups, but these new states did not evolve into democratic regimes.

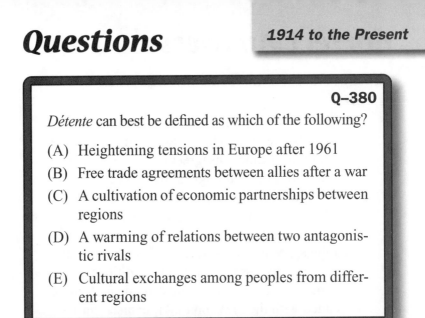

Q–380

Détente can best be defined as which of the following?

(A) Heightening tensions in Europe after 1961

(B) Free trade agreements between allies after a war

(C) A cultivation of economic partnerships between regions

(D) A warming of relations between two antagonistic rivals

(E) Cultural exchanges among peoples from different regions

Your Answer _____

Correct Answers

A–380

(D) The Cold War period saw rising and falling tensions between the United States and the Soviet Union over time. Disagreements over Germany and Cuba almost brought about world war in the 1940s and 1960s, respectively. In the 1970s, relations had improved so that arms agreements and technological exchanges were possible. Joint space missions were carried out, and some began to discuss the end of the traditional enmity between communism and capitalism. Détente ended with the invasion of Afghanistan in 1979 by the Soviet Union, after which the United States boycotted the Moscow Olympics and cut off grain exports to the Soviet Union.

Q–381

The women's movement of the 1960s and 1970s sought which of the following goals?

I. Legal equality for men and women

II. Equal opportunity in the work place

III. Greater roles in the political arena

IV. More money for women participating in interscholastic sports than that received by men in interscholastic sports

(A) II, III, and IV only

(B) I and II only

(C) I, II, and IV only

(D) I, II, and III only

(E) I, III, and IV only

Your Answer _____

_____

Correct Answers

A–381

(D) The women's movement, or feminism, sought basic equality with men in many different arenas. In sports, laws were sponsored so that high schools had to spend the same amount of money on their sports programs for females as for males. The opportunity to advance professionally in all fields was another goal of the movement. Greater participation in the political work of the nation strove to give more women representation in local and national government. Attempts to break the old stereotypes of women being weaker or less able were articulated by feminists.

Q-382

Mass marketing combined with a global mass media has led to which of the following around the world?

(A) Chinese has become the de facto world language.

(B) Global pop culture has been heavily influenced by the West.

(C) Corporations have become less influential worldwide.

(D) Art and literature have become more mono-cultural.

(E) Profits for multinational companies have declined.

Your Answer _____

Q-383

Conflicts in Africa after 1960 have been made more deadly by the availability of

(A) birth control methods imported from Europe

(B) small arms and light weapons

(C) nuclear weapons from the West

(D) oil in certain nations

(E) chemical weapons from the United States

Your Answer _____

Correct Answers

A–382

(B) The media, in the form of television, radio, the Internet, and film, have become more available internationally due to advances in technology. Corporations that sell to many different countries advertise to and influence people across the globe. Some have complained that American and Western cultures have become too powerful because they sell food and fashion to many people. Art and literature has become more diverse and multicultural to reflect populations in many nations.

A–383

(B) Intertribal and civil wars have been common in Africa since decolonization. Forced drafting of young people into armies and militias has been noted in various parts of the continent. The availability of small arms in the form of automatic rifles and rocket-propelled grenades (RPGs) has meant higher death rates and instability throughout Africa. African nations that are rich in mineral resources have been able to spend millions of dollars on small arms to keep their hold on power.

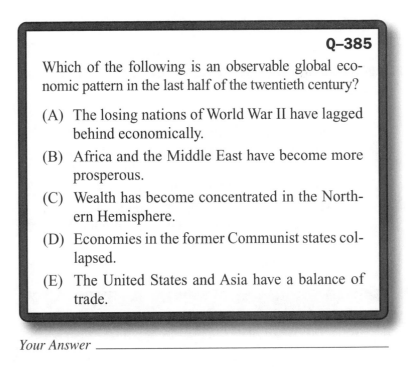

Q–384

Which of the following nations possessed nuclear weapons capability by 1970?

(A) China and France
(B) India and Vietnam
(C) South Africa and Great Britain
(D) Russia and Poland
(E) The United States and Canada

Your Answer _____

Q–385

Which of the following is an observable global economic pattern in the last half of the twentieth century?

(A) The losing nations of World War II have lagged behind economically.
(B) Africa and the Middle East have become more prosperous.
(C) Wealth has become concentrated in the Northern Hemisphere.
(D) Economies in the former Communist states collapsed.
(E) The United States and Asia have a balance of trade.

Your Answer _____

Correct Answers

A–384

(A) World War II saw the development of atomic (nuclear) weapons by the United States, and the United States used them to end the war. After the war, the Soviet Union (Russia) tested its own nuclear weapons, which framed the rest of the Cold War. Britain and France successfully tested nuclear weapons in the 1950s to join the "nuclear club." The People's Republic of China joined the nuclear club in 1964. Since 1970, other nations such as India have also exploded a nuclear device.

A–385

(C) Since the Age of Discovery, the leading economies of the world were northern European nations, which were joined later by the United States and Japan. Today, the leading economies are all located in the Northern Hemisphere, while many of the poorer nations are in the Southern Hemisphere. This geographical dichotomy has created a divide between the north and the south.

Q–386

How did the Cold War influence regional conflicts after 1949?

(A) The United Nations was able to defeat communism in Korea.

(B) The United States and the Soviet Union fought each other indirectly through client states.

(C) American forces intervened directly in Latin American revolutions.

(D) The Soviet Union created protectorates throughout Africa.

(E) Israel remained nonaligned until the 1980s.

Your Answer _____

Q–387

Which of the following describes the legal trend for indigenous native peoples in the twentieth century?

(A) More land rights and autonomy have been gained.

(B) Systematic persecution has led to many deaths.

(C) Native groups have seceded to form independent countries.

(D) Europeans have refused to apologize for past abuses.

(E) Disease continues to ravage tribal peoples.

Your Answer _____

Correct Answers

A–386

(B) Starting with the Korean conflict, the United States became involved in various conflicts in which it opposed communist nations who were supplied by the Soviet Union. This happened in Korea, Vietnam, Cuba, and also the Middle East into the 1980s.

A–387

(A) In past centuries, native peoples have been devastated by disease and have lost large tracts of land to the settlers from Europe. In recent decades, however, governments from Australia to Canada, to Mexico, have come to recognize the rights of indigenous peoples and even apologized for the conflicts of the past. Indigenous peoples have been given more rights to land and economic autonomy within nation-states. Tribal groups can regulate themselves and profit from selling goods not available outside their zones of control.

Q-388

The world energy crisis of the early 1970s was caused in part by

(A) the assassination of Prime Minister Rabin in Israel
(B) tensions in the Middle East and increasing fuel consumption in the West
(C) the Vietnam War
(D) Pan-Arab nationalism promoted by Nasser
(E) American support for a Palestinian state

Your Answer _____

Q-389

The democratic camp is growing stronger every day. The anti-democratic camp headed by America was founded at the end of World War II. The Americans have become the leaders of the imperialist and reactionary forces in the world. France and Britain are their lackeys . . .

—Ho Chi Minh, 1953

The quotation above by Ho Chi Minh was most influenced by

(A) fascist ideology
(B) constitutionalism
(C) postmodern internationalism
(D) Marxist-Leninism
(E) Buddhist thought

Your Answer _____

Correct Answers

A–388

(B) Consumption of petroleum rose steadily in the industrial West throughout the twentieth century. After World War II, major oil corporations searched for and found large reserves in the Middle East and South America. The creation of the state of Israel created tensions between Zionist Israel and neighboring Arab nations. The largest oil producer was also Saudi Arabia, and this fact set the stage for the use of petroleum as an economic weapon. Even with the discovery of more American oil in Alaska, the United States had to import large quantities of Middle Eastern petroleum. After the fourth war in four decades between Israel and Arab nations bent on its destruction, Saudi Arabia cut back on production of oil, which led to a rise in crude petroleum prices worldwide.

A–389

(D) Ho Chi Minh is the father of modern Vietnam who had became a Marxist revolutionary by the 1950s. He aligned himself with world communism and sought help from both Soviet Russia and China after 1949. Although he was also a nationalist, Ho believed in the world revolution that Marx had predicted and Lenin sought to further. His struggle against French imperialism and American anticommunism forced him to fight all his life until his death in 1969. By identifying the United States as the leading imperialistic power, he used the language of Lenin, Stalin, and Mao to oppose the capitalist West.

Q–390

Most agricultural workers in mid-twentieth-century China were

(A) sharecroppers
(B) landless serfs
(C) slaves
(D) prosperous small family farmers
(E) free peasants

Your Answer _____

_____

Q–391

Which of the following countries or regions led the world in the production of wheat in 1950?

(A) The Soviet Union
(B) France
(C) Canada
(D) The United States
(E) Argentina

Your Answer _____

_____

Correct Answers

A–390

(E) China was populated mostly by rural farm workers in the first half of the twentieth century. These farmer/peasants were free but often barely survived working the land for other people. Sixty-five percent of all arable land was owned by less than 10 percent of the total population. This meant that peasants rented the land and worked to provide for their families. Between rent and high taxes paid to the government, many families worked long hours to survive. One lean harvest might mean starvation. Add disease and natural disasters, and one can see the great challenge of twentieth-century rural life in China.

A–391

(D) After World War II, while much of the world recovered from the destruction on multiple continents, the United States was the leading producer of wheat. The breadbasket of America has been in the middle states of Kansas, Colorado, North Dakota, and Montana. After the 1960s, China and India were able to surpass the United States in wheat cultivation and production.

Q–392

The photo above shows the Arc de Triomphe located in Paris. The monument is an example of

(A) postmodern building style

(B) nationalist European architecture

(C) German influence

(D) the wealth created by imperialism

(E) Buddhist temple architecture

Your Answer _____

_____

Correct Answers

A–392

(B) The Arc de Triomphe was built by Napoleon and has occupied a special place in French history ever since. In defeat and victory, the French have seen their own troops and those of conquering nations march through and past the famous monument. It represents French military nationalism and recalls the glories of French history.

Questions

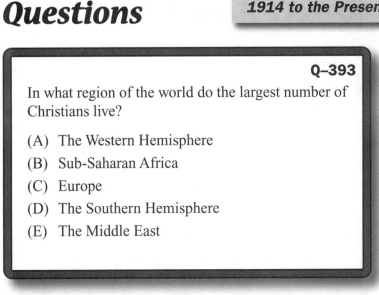

Q–393

In what region of the world do the largest number of Christians live?

(A) The Western Hemisphere

(B) Sub-Saharan Africa

(C) Europe

(D) The Southern Hemisphere

(E) The Middle East

Your Answer _____

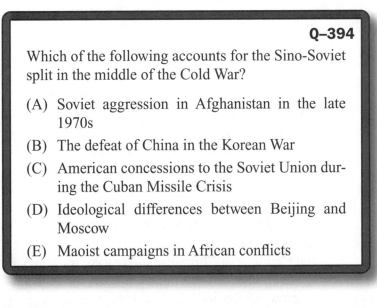

Q–394

Which of the following accounts for the Sino-Soviet split in the middle of the Cold War?

(A) Soviet aggression in Afghanistan in the late 1970s

(B) The defeat of China in the Korean War

(C) American concessions to the Soviet Union during the Cuban Missile Crisis

(D) Ideological differences between Beijing and Moscow

(E) Maoist campaigns in African conflicts

Your Answer _____

Correct Answers

A–393

(A) Christians make up more than 80 percent of the populations of nations such as Brazil, the United States, and Mexico. While many Christians also live in nations such as the Philippines and France, there are more followers of the Christian faith in the Western Hemisphere than in any other region.

A–394

(D) After the death of Stalin, Mao felt less deferential toward Moscow in his revolutionary thinking. Mao was a first-generation revolutionary, while the Soviet leadership was made up of second-generation Marxists. The World War II experience was interpreted differently by the two Communist nations, and Mao thought that Soviet leaders were becoming less fervent in their view of world revolution. These differing views of Marxism led to different approaches in opposing the West after 1965. By 1969, Soviet and Communist Chinese soldiers were shooting at one another on their mutual border, which led to growing tensions between the two nuclear powers.

Questions

Q–395

Which of the following are offshoots of monotheistic religions in the world?

(A) Mahayana and Lamaist Buddhism

(B) Jainism and Sikhism

(C) Catholicism and Protestantism

(D) Taoism and Shintoism

(E) Zoroastrianism and animism

Your Answer _____

_____

Q–396

The breakup of the Soviet Union after 1989 can be attributed in part to

(A) Cold War success in Afghanistan

(B) arms agreements with the United States

(C) new nationalist movements within the Soviet Union

(D) oppressive Politburo policies

(E) pressure from the United Nations to liberalize immigration policies

Your Answer _____

_____

Correct Answers

A–395

(C) Each of the three monotheisms have experienced divisions over the centuries. Judaism has divided into orthodox and more liberal groupings, while Christianity split into Eastern and Western branches. Europe further divided itself into Catholic and Protestant churches after 1500. These Christian organizations have since transplanted themselves throughout the world. Islam created two branches after the death of Mohammed, when some supported the leadership of the prophet's son-in-law, Ali.

A–396

(C) The Soviet Union had always been a diverse mix of peoples in Europe and Asia. The totalitarian dictatorship of Stalin kept it together before and after World War II. As the Politburo liberalized certain policies in the 1980s, satellite nations and ethnic groups within the Soviet Union began to speak out for more freedom. Very rapidly, pieces of the Soviet Union broke away to create new nations such as Kazakhstan, Ukraine, and Moldova.

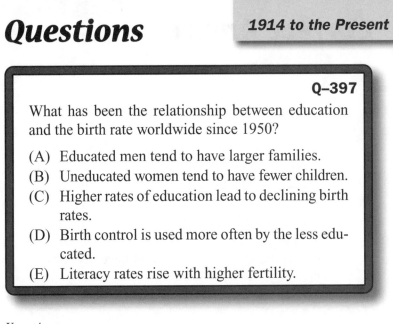

Q–397

What has been the relationship between education and the birth rate worldwide since 1950?

(A) Educated men tend to have larger families.

(B) Uneducated women tend to have fewer children.

(C) Higher rates of education lead to declining birth rates.

(D) Birth control is used more often by the less educated.

(E) Literacy rates rise with higher fertility.

Your Answer _____

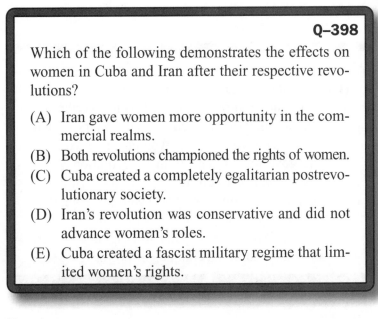

Q–398

Which of the following demonstrates the effects on women in Cuba and Iran after their respective revolutions?

(A) Iran gave women more opportunity in the commercial realms.

(B) Both revolutions championed the rights of women.

(C) Cuba created a completely egalitarian postrevolutionary society.

(D) Iran's revolution was conservative and did not advance women's roles.

(E) Cuba created a fascist military regime that limited women's rights.

Your Answer _____

Correct Answers

A–397

(C) Nations with higher literacy and education rates have seen declining marriage and birth rates. Most notable are nations with effective centralized education systems, such as Japan and France, which are seeing birth rates sink below zero population growth (ZPG). Women in countries with high illiteracy have more children and get married earlier. Nations with a well-educated population marry later and have fewer children.

A–398

(D) The Iranian and Cuban revolutions were quite different from one another. Castro overthrew a corrupt dictator and established a Marxist state that attempted to grant women more voice in the government. The Iranian revolution was a theological reaction against the modernization of the shah's regime. The ayatollah sought to create an Islamic republic that resembled a theocracy. Women had rather few rights and were not included in the councils of power.

Questions

Q–399

Wars in Indochina and Afghanistan highlighted what military lessons in the twentieth century?

(A) High-tech weaponry could subdue an insurgent movement.

(B) Strategic bombing was sufficient to defeat an enemy.

(C) Guerrilla warfare could prevail against high-tech armies.

(D) Military juntas are vulnerable to communist insurgencies.

(E) Postcolonial governments cannot defeat Western armies.

Your Answer _____

Q–400

Which of the following is an outcome of the end of the Cold War after 1989?

(A) Tensions in the Middle East diminished.

(B) Former Communist countries fragmented, which resulted in new nations.

(C) Nations gave up their nuclear arsenals.

(D) China began to allow internal criticism from its citizens.

(E) Indian-Pakistani tensions erupted in war.

Your Answer _____

Correct Answers

A–399

(C) Both wars in Vietnam and Afghanistan saw large armies from powerful nations defeated by local guerrilla insurgent movements. Superior firepower and air cover were not able to subdue well-organized fighters using mountains or jungles as their cover. Billions of dollars were spent by the United States in the 1960s and by the Soviet Union in the 1980s to defeat smaller but determined local forces. Long frustrating campaigns resulted, with high casualties on both sides. These long wars of attrition eventually saw the departure of the better-equipped foreign forces.

A–400

(B) The end of the Cold War came quickly and resulted in nations breaking into pieces. The former Soviet Union became known as the Commonwealth of Independent States, but this was merely a transition before new nations came into being. Likewise, Yugoslavia broke into numerous pieces, and nations such as Serbia, Slovenia, and Macedonia eventually came into being. After 1990, more than ten new nations were created from the former Communist states.

Take Test-Readiness Quiz 4 on CD
(to review questions 299–400)

Blank Cards for *Your Own Questions*

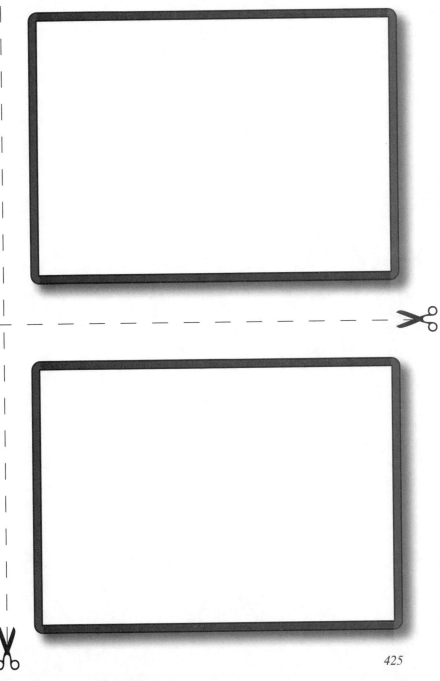

Correct Answers

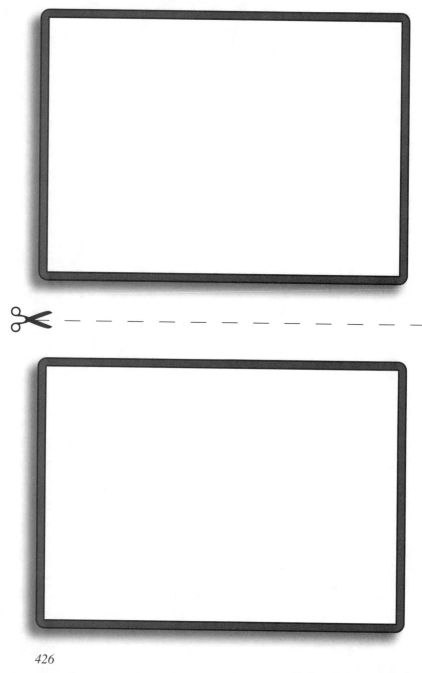

Blank Cards for
Your Own Questions

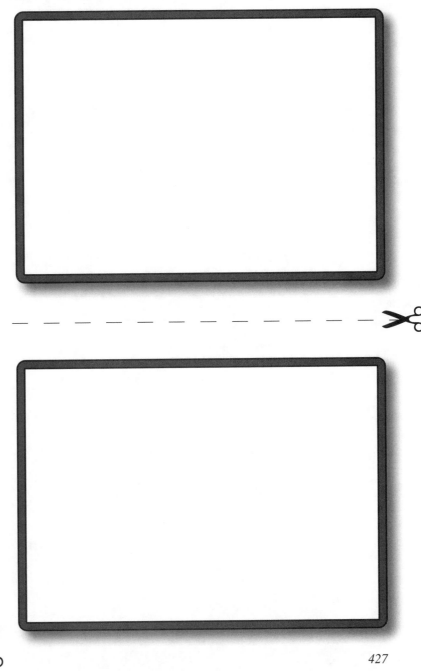

Correct Answers

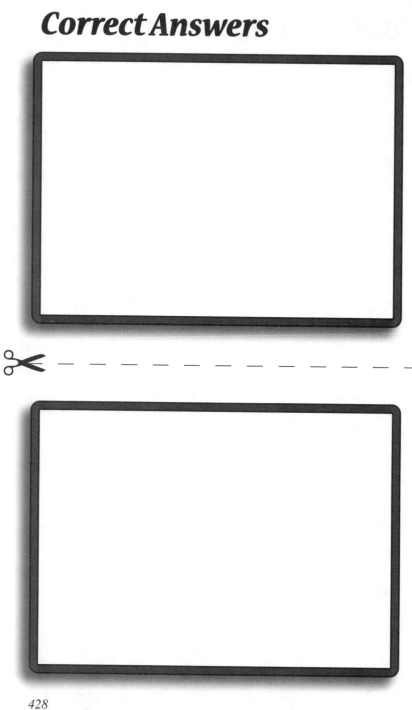

Index

Index

[Note: Numbers in the Index refer to question numbers.]

[Note: Numbers in the Index refer to question numbers.]

Index

[Note: Numbers in the Index refer to question numbers.]

Index

Image Acknowledgments: